D0032628

THE
APPLE
CIDER
VINEGAR
COMPANION

THE APPLE CIDER VINEGAR COMPANION

Simple Ways to
Use Nature's Miracle Cure

SUZY SCHERR

The Countryman Press
A division of W. W. Norton & Company
Independent Publishers Since 1923

Photo Credits:
Page viii, 10, 11: © sasimoto/Shutterstock.com; 4: © Es75/Shutterstock.com; 15, 153, 155: © ThamKC/Shutterstock.com; 16: © Marie C Fields/Shutterstock.com; 20, 23, 105: © Africa Studio/Shutterstock.com; 24: © puchan/iStockphoto.com; 26: © Diane Diederich/ iStockphoto.com; 28: © Evgeny Karandaev/Shutterstock.com; 29, 31: © vanillaechoes/ Shutterstock.com; 32: © deepblue/Shutterstock.com; 33: © Julia Sudnitskaya/ Shutterstock.com; 34: © Chris Gramly/iStockphoto.com; 37: © Maria-Lapina/iStockphoto .com; 41: © HandmadePictures/iStockphoto.com; 43: © marysckin/Shutterstock.com; 45: © 13Smile/Shutterstock.com; 47: © Tim UR/Shutterstock.com; 48: © stockphoto-graf/ Shutterstock.com; 52: © Jayme Burrows/Shutterstock.com; 53: © sarsmis/Shutterstock .com; 55, 60: © Eva Gruendemann/Shutterstock.com; 56: © Mariha-kitchen/iStockphoto .com; 59: © Joshua Resnick/Shutterstock.com; 65: © Monticello/Shutterstock.com; 66: © Robyn Mackenzie/Shutterstock.com; 69: © Catherine Murray/Shutterstock .com; 70, 132: © Brent Hofacker/Shutterstock.com; 73: © farbled/Shutterstock.com; 80: © VankaD/iStockphoto.com; 83: © iso_petrov/iStockphoto.com; 84: © AnjelikaGr/ Shutterstock.com; 87: © sivanadar/Shutterstock.com; 88: © neil langan/Shutterstock .com; 95: © Tiger Images/Shutterstock.com; 101: © BklynRod/iStockphoto.com; 103: © timages/Shutterstock.com; 112: © sveta_zarzamora/iStockphoto.com; 115: © Anna Pustynnikova/iStockphoto.com; 116: © Evgenialevi/Shutterstock.com; 119: © Pinkcandy/Shutterstock.com; 120: © mama_mia/Shutterstock.com; 123: © George Dolgikh/Shutterstock.com; 125: © Gayvoronskaya_Yana/Shutterstock.com; 126: © Lauri Patterson/iStockphoto.com; 131: © showcake/Shutterstock.com; 137: © ffolas/ Shutterstock.com; 138: © Sean Wandzilak/Shutterstock.com; 140: © Savas Keskiner/ iStockphoto.com; 143: © Christian Jung/Shutterstock.com; 150: © Milosz_G/Shutterstock .com; 163: © g-stocksstudio/iStockphoto.com

Copyright © 2016 by Suzy Scherr

All rights reserved
Printed in the United States of America

For information about permission to reproduce selections from this book, write to Permissions, The Countryman Press, 500 Fifth Avenue, New York, NY 10110

For information about special discounts for bulk purchases, please contact W. W. Norton Special Sales at specialsales@wwnorton.com or 800-233-4830

Library of Congress Cataloging-in-Publication Data

Names: Scherr, Suzy, author.
Title: The apple cider vinegar companion : simple ways to use nature's miracle cure / Suzy Scherr.
Description: Woodstock, VT : Countryman Press, a division of W. W. Norton & Company, [2016] | Includes index.
Identifiers: LCCN 2016006998 | ISBN 9781581573602 (pbk.)
Subjects: LCSH: Cider vinegar—Therapeutic use. | Cider vinegar—Health aspects. | Functional foods. | Cooking (Vinegar) | LCGFT: Cookbooks.
Classification: LCC RM666.V55 S34 2016 | DDC 615.3/2373—dc23 LC record available at https://lccn.loc.gov/2016006998

The Countryman Press
www.countrymanpress.com

A division of W. W. Norton & Company, Inc.
500 Fifth Avenue, New York, NY 10110
www.wwnorton.com

10 9 8 7 6 5 4 3 2 1

For my family.

CONTENTS

INTRODUCTION

I want you to know that I am a real person: a busy chef and mom, living a somewhat-chaotic-but-largely-fun life with a husband and two small kids in a moderately cluttered, wholly imperfect, but warm and comfortable home. If you knew me, you'd probably describe me as a something of a fun-loving pragmatist in the kitchen. The food I cook is real food. It is unfussy, unpretentious, accessible food. I use widely familiar ingredients and try to make dishes that are interesting, fun, healthy, and delicious. I've never been into gimmicks when it comes to eating and health, holding firm to the belief that moderation is best and that consuming *real* food, even carbs (mostly good ones), even dessert (preferably homemade), is part of what makes life worth living. I don't really believe in nutritional panaceas; terms like *superfood*, *detox*, and *clean eating* aren't part of my everyday vernacular.

So . . . who was that groggy woman in my kitchen the other morning, joylessly choking down a tall glass of sludgy smoothie, so thick with pulverized kale that it barely passed through the straw? Yeah, that was me—because kale is, apparently, the answer to everything.

Okay, so I'm not impervious to food trends, but for the most part, I believe that a balanced diet—heavy on the green stuff, easy on the junk—is all we need to keep our system in working order. That and a little (not-so) secret weapon called apple cider vinegar.

Apple cider vinegar is a real-deal miracle product. Prepare to become a hard-core believer in its delicious flavor, myriad household uses, and fabulous health benefits. You're about to join generations upon generations of devotees who have sworn by apple cider vinegar—cooking with it, swigging it by the spoonful, and using it as a remedy for just about any ailment. You'll be making pickles with it, cleaning your house with it, killing garden weeds with it, making salad dressing with it, and repelling fruit flies with it. You'll use it to naturally freshen your breath, ease your sore throats, and soothe your upset stomachs. Remember the dad from the movie *My Big Fat Greek Wedding*, who exalted Windex as a cure for anything and everything, running around with a spray bottle and the mantra, "Put some Windex on it!" (As in: Got a scratch on your elbow? Put some Windex on it! Got a pimple? Put some Windex on it!)? Well, you're about to become that dad, except you'll be saying, "Put some apple cider vinegar on it!" You'll see.

While it's true that apple cider vinegar is my go-to product for all manner of kitchen, health, and household uses, it wasn't always that way. This book could just as easily have been called *Confessions of a Reformed Product Hoarder*. If you're like I was, at one point or another in your life you, too, have had cabinets and drawers full of half-used bottles, tubs, and packets containing household and personal care products. Look under the sink in the kitchen, in your laundry room, in the medicine cabinet, in the pantry, and I bet you'll find some pretty expensive and fairly ineffective stuff lying around: lotions and potions, tablets and capsules, all promising to lower your cholesterol, boost your energy, brighten your skin, sparkle your windows, whiten your teeth, feed your plants, and more. The problem I found with so many of those supposed miracle products, aside from the fact that many of them don't work all that well, is that they're full of unpronounceable, chemical-laden ingredients and involve enough excess packaging to fill a jumbo-size dumpster. Not exactly what I'd call green living. Apple cider vinegar, on the other hand, is completely natural and, since it can do pretty much *anything*, it replaces tons of the products you buy regularly, eliminating manufactured packaging left and right and saving you money. Think about it: apple cider vinegar's healing, cleaning, freshening, fortifying, preserving, and flavoring power leaves you with extra cabinet space *and* extra money. I'm a chef, not an economist, but to me that clearly equates to being able to splurge on more kitchen gadgets. Extra money + extra space = reason enough to shop the local cookware store. Or is that just me? Anyway, apple cider vinegar is an incredible all-in-one product that will really and truly change the way you live. That's why I created this book: to show you easy and effective ways to incorporate apple cider vinegar into your lifestyle.

GETTING STARTED WITH APPLE CIDER VINEGAR

Apple cider vinegar has been around for centuries. It's old school. I'm talking Hippocrates-the-father-of-modern-medicine old school. He started prescribing it around 400 BC, usually combined with honey, to treat all sorts of ailments. Roman armies and samurai warriors supposedly cared for their wounds with apple cider vinegar and administered it as a tonic to energize troops. For generations, folk medicine has enlisted apple cider vinegar to treat everything from diabetes to acid reflux, the common cold to warts, cancer, arthritis, toenail fungus, bad breath, high cholesterol, poison ivy, urinary tract infections, and even head lice! In other words, apple cider vinegar is one of the oldest, most-prized, and trusted remedies in history. For generations every grandmother knew dozens of ways apple cider vinegar could be used. I don't know about your grandmother, but taking advice from mine was usually the right thing to do.

What *Is* Apple Cider Vinegar and Why Should You Be Using It Every Day?

I know you're familiar with vinegar. Chances are you've used basic, widely available distilled white vinegar for cooking, cleaning, or—at the very least—dyeing Easter eggs or erupting baking soda volcanoes in science class. Perhaps you've sprinkled malt vinegar on fish and chips or dressed a salad with dark and syrupy balsamic vinegar or bracing red wine vinegar. All vinegar, regardless of its variety, is formed through fermentation, and is named from the French *vin aigre*, which means "sour wine." If you take apples and ferment them with the right bacteria, first the concoction will turn alcoholic (becoming hard cider, essentially). Then, if fermented further, the alcohol turns into acetic and malic acids, the mixture sours, and the resulting liquid is multitasking, all natural, inexpensive, antifungal, antibacterial, antiviral, fat-burning, cholesterol-lowering, immunity-boosting apple cider vinegar. It will improve your health and your home inside and out. It is a liquid rock star. But there is a caveat and here it is:

> *When talking about the health benefits of apple cider vinegar, I'm referring to a specific type of apple cider vinegar: raw and unpasteurized.*

While most commercial apple cider vinegars are pasteurized, clear solutions, it is only the unfiltered, raw variety that has the beneficial bacteria, enzymes, and minerals that make it such a health-promoting solution. The reason?

The mother: the strandlike sediment or gnarly blob you'll see floating at the bottom of a bottle of raw apple cider vinegar. Sounds unpleasant, but it's actually a really important part of what makes apple cider vinegar so incredible. The mother is basically a combination of cellulose and bacteria that is formed during the fermentation process. While she may look grungy and gruesome, the mother contains raw enzymes and friendly bacteria that promote healing. Word to your mother.

Buying and Storing Apple Cider Vinegar

You can find raw apple cider vinegar at most health food stores or in the natural foods section of your local grocery store. In fact, if the vinegar is raw and unpasteurized, it will likely say "with the mother" right there on the label. If so, you can be sure you're getting some bodacious apple cider vinegar, as opposed to many mass-produced vinegars, which are highly attenuated through the use of heat and chemicals. In other words, they're manufactured, not naturally fermented.

Apple cider vinegar should be stored in a relatively cool spot, out of direct sunlight. I keep mine in the pantry. Because of the high acidity levels, there's no need to refrigerate apple cider vinegar, as it won't become moldy—but you should follow the expiration date on your store-bought vinegar to ensure that it is at its best.

DIY Homemade Apple Cider Vinegar

Apple cider vinegar is surprisingly easy and almost unimaginably inexpensive to make at home, requiring little more than apples, time, a knife, and a jar. That's basically it. I usually use scraps (peels and cores) that I store in the fridge until I'm ready to make a batch of apple cider vinegar, so the whole shebang is almost free. It's a simple process that results in something quite delicious—and, of course, healthy, cleansing, antibacterial, antiviral, and all that really important stuff I've managed to beat you over the head with up until this point. But life is short and deliciousness matters, so on with it:

YOU WILL NEED:

3 small apples, washed and roughly chopped, or the peels and cores from 6 or 7 small apples

3 teaspoons sugar or honey

Filtered or distilled water to cover

1. Place the apple pieces in a clean quart-size jar.

2. In a small bowl, combine the sugar with 1 cup of water and pour over the apples, covering completely. The apples must be completely submerged in water to prevent the growth of mold, so if you find that you don't have enough liquid in the jar, add an additional ½ tablespoon of sugar and ½ cup of water. If necessary, place an upturned lid from another smaller jar on top of the apples to keep them submerged.

3. Cover the jar with a paper towel, cheesecloth, or coffee filter and secure it with a rubber band or piece of twine.

4. Place the jar in a warm, dark place for 2 to 3 weeks. At this point, you'll probably notice some fizz or bubbles, which means everything's working according to plan!

5. Strain out the liquid and discard the solids.

6. Return the liquid to the jar and cover again as before.

7. Allow the liquid to ferment in a dark place for 4 to 6 weeks, tasting it once a week.

8. Once it reaches an acidity and flavor you like (you'll know when it's become vinegar), either cap the jar with a lid or transfer it to another bottle with a lid.

Congratulations! You've just made apple cider vinegar!

A Bit of Common Sense

Most people won't experience adverse side effects from apple cider vinegar, but please keep in mind apple cider vinegar is quite acidic, so it can wear away tooth enamel and do a number on your stomach if taken at full strength on a regular basis. Pregnant or nursing mothers should speak with their doctor before starting an apple cider vinegar regimen. Apple cider vinegar may interact with certain diabetic and heart medications. You should speak with your doctor before starting a long-term regimen of apple cider vinegar to make certain that it is appropriate for you.

CLEVER WAYS TO USE APPLE CIDER VINEGAR AT HOME

This chapter will teach you everyday ways to keep your family and home healthy, happy, sparkling, and shiny with apple cider vinegar. I'll share the remedies, tricks, and tips that I use in my own home as well as recipes (old-fashioned and newfangled), which you will easily master, regardless of your experience as a cook.

HEALTH AND WELLNESS

SORE THROAT SOOTHER

So often a sore throat seems to come out of nowhere—you go to sleep feeling fine and wake up in the morning barely able to swallow. Whether caused by infection or irritant, try to treat

your sore throat as soon as it starts to rear its ugly head or bother yours. Apple cider vinegar's high levels of acidity can kill bacteria efficiently, and when mixed with honey it can really help ease even the scratchiest, angriest of sore throats. Here are a couple of home remedies:

¼ cup honey

¼ cup apple cider vinegar

In a small bowl or jar, combine the honey and apple cider vinegar and take a tablespoon at a time every 4 hours, or as needed to ease the pain.

Or, try this:

1 tablespoon apple cider vinegar

8 ounces warm water

Combine the vinegar and water in a glass or mug; gargle several times a day.

HOMEMADE COUGH AND COLD SYRUP

With only a handful of pantry ingredients and a few minutes' effort, this homemade cough and cold syrup can be sitting on our counter in no time, arming you against cold and flu season. It's a spicy-yet-soothing syrup, effective at calming a cough and soothing a sore throat. Cayenne pepper, honey, and ginger are all natural expectorants, which means they help loosen mucus from the lungs, making you more comfortable. Cayenne is also an effective decongestant, thanks to the chemical capsaicin, which gives spicy peppers their heat and helps relieve swelling and inflammation in the nasal passages. Apple cider vinegar helps thin out nasal secretions, making it easier to drain the mucus so you can breathe. In other words: Ahhh. Finally.

2 tablespoons apple cider vinegar

2 tablespoons honey

2 tablespoons water

¼ teaspoon cayenne pepper

¼ teaspoon ground ginger

1. Combine all the ingredients in a small jar and shake to combine.

2. Store in a cool, dark place.

3. Shake well before using; take 1 to 2 tablespoons as needed to relieve symptoms. If desired, warm the mixture slightly before taking.

ITCHY SKIN RELIEVER

Around here, summer is referred to as "the season of the itch." From sunburns to bug bites, and heat rashes to poison ivy, it seems we're a pretty scratchy bunch when the weather heats up. My husband claims he has "sweet meat," which is why mosquitoes love him—poor guy. Thankfully, apple cider vinegar is a really effective way to calm the "itchies." It's great for rashes, allergies, bug bites, peeling sunburns, dry skin, and other irritations. Not only is it a natural virus and germ fighter, apple cider vinegar helps restore skin's natural pH balance, which can really help smooth out dry patches and relieve redness. As it turns out, our skin is naturally acidic, with a pH value of around 5.5. Many cleansers and lotions strip away this acidity, making our skin susceptible to germs and irritants. But apple cider vinegar, which contains not only acid but also many beneficial enzymes, can help maintain skin's natural pH level. In fact, we use it year-round, since dry air and intense cold in winter can parch our skin, too. Whatever the season, here's how to treat itchy skin:

As a topical treatment

Cotton balls, gauze, or cotton swabs
Apple cider vinegar

1. Saturate a cotton ball, gauze, or a cotton swab with the undiluted vinegar.

2. Dab directly on itchy areas. It is an especially effective spot treatment for bug bites.

For severely itchy skin

½ cup apple cider vinegar
½ cup cornstarch

1. In a small bowl, combine the vinegar and cornstarch to make a paste.

2. Apply the paste liberally to the affected areas.

For larger areas or all-over itching

2 to 3 cups apple cider vinegar
Bathtub full of warm water

Add the vinegar to a freshly drawn bath and soak for 15 to 30 minutes.

For athlete's foot

5 cups apple cider vinegar
1 gallon water

1. Combine the vinegar and water in a large basin or bowl.

2. Soak the feet for at least 10 minutes to help relieve the itching and scaling of athlete's foot.

TUMMY TAMER

I do my best to eat a balanced diet; drink plenty of water; take in the recommended amount of fiber; and consume dairy, alcohol, caffeine, and sugar in moderation. But sometimes—usually due to stress, eating on the go, or a day or two of loving food just a little too much—I end up in a state that can be characterized only as "gastrointestinally challenged." When this happens, I reach for apple cider vinegar, which I like to think of as my intestinal reset button. Because the vinegar mimics the acidic environment of the stomach and helps food to break down, it effectively reduces symptoms of reflux, heartburn, gas, bloating, abdominal pain and cramping, and constipation—they're often caused by having too little stomach acid rather than too much. It also helps considerably with diarrhea: pectin, iron, and acetic acid, which all occur naturally in raw apple cider vinegar, combine to form a fibrous gel that helps soothe an irritated digestive tract and bulk up stool to slow things down.

To ease indigestion

1 cup cool or room-temperature water

2 to 4 teaspoons apple cider vinegar, depending on the severity of your discomfort

1. Combine the water and vinegar in a glass.

2. Sip the drink slowly, over a period of 20 to 30 minutes. Relief should come gradually over this period.

To soothe a stomachache and/or find immediate relief from constipation

1 cup cool or room-temperature water

1 tablespoon apple cider vinegar

1. Combine the water and vinegar in a glass.

2. Sip over a period of 30 minutes.

3. To prevent future bouts of constipation, drink this mixture up to three times daily.

To overcome diarrhea

1 cup warm water

1 to 2 tablespoons apple cider vinegar

1. Combine the water and vinegar in a glass or mug.

2. Drink the mixture over a period of 15 minutes.

3. Repeat as frequently as once an hour until the diarrhea subsides.

POSTWORKOUT MUSCLE SOAK

An especially tough workout really does hurt so good. But sometimes—often the next day—it just hurts. Not so good. There are a few theories as to the cause of those after-the-fact aches and pains, known medically as delayed onset muscle soreness. Some suggest that lactic acid buildup causes a shift in muscle pH, causing soreness during movement. Others point to tiny, microscopic tears in the muscle tissue. Either way, a bath laced with apple cider vinegar will calm inflammation, improve blood flow, and ease soreness.

To make a soothing soak for allover aches and pains

2 to 4 cups apple cider vinegar
Bathtub full of warm water

1. Add the vinegar to the warm bath water.

2. Soak for 30 to 60 minutes.

Note: Try adding a handful of bruised mint or eucalyptus leaves to the water for an extra-refreshing and invigorating bath

To soothe a tired or overworked muscle

1 cup apple cider vinegar

1 cup water

1 rag

1. Combine the vinegar and water in a large bowl or basin, then soak the rag in the mixture.

2. Wring out the rag and place on the affected area, then cover with plastic wrap and a towel. Leave it on for 15 to 20 minutes.

ENERGY BOOSTER

The next time you need a jolt of energy, say around three p.m., when your eyelids begin to feel like lead and your head begins, ever so slowly, to descend gently towards your keyboard, try skipping your usual afternoon soda, coffee, or über-caffeinated energy drink. Those "pick-me-ups" offer only a short-term buzz and almost no nutritional benefit. Instead, stop that afternoon snooze-fest before it starts with an all-natural energy drink that's refreshing, hydrating, and full of beneficial enzymes, vitamins, and minerals.

2 teaspoons apple cider vinegar
2 cups sparkling or still water

1. Combine the vinegar and water in a tall glass.

2. Sip and enjoy!

HICCUP CURE

Hic. Hic. Hic. . . . Forget holding your breath, drinking a glass of water upside down, breathing into a paper bag, or eating a spoonful of sugar. The surest, quickest way to cure a pesky case of the hiccups is to reach for your trusty stash of raw apple cider vinegar. Since hiccups are often caused by either low stomach acid (which slows the digestion of protein) or by simply overdoing it at mealtime, apple cider vinegar can be a great solution. It resets the acid balance in your stomach and eases those annoying spasms of the diaphragm.

1 teaspoon apple cider vinegar

1 cup warm water

1. Combine the vinegar and water in a glass.

2. Sip slowly.

3. And if that doesn't work, try whistling "Yankee Doodle Dandy" through a straw while standing on your head.

COOKING

In cooking, I like how apple cider vinegar's predominantly sour flavor balances with its fruity sweetness. It is incredibly versatile and, as these recipes highlight, it lends itself well to marinades, chutneys, salads, and dressings, where it adds brightness and that little . . . extra something. It's a natural complement to apples, pears, cabbage, onions, garlic, ginger, and a variety of meats. It adds amazing lift and airiness to baked goods, particularly when combined with baking soda. And it allows cooks of all skill levels to turn out some incredible, interesting pickles in a relatively short amount of time. Moreover, as a beverage, it offers well-proven health benefits and incredible refreshment in one fell swoop. Some of the recipes here are newfangled, such as Maple Bourbon Carrot and Parsnip Pickles (pages 98–99), but because apple cider vinegar has been around for so long, I couldn't overlook age-old gems, such as Eggless Chocolate Bundt Cake (pages 136–37) and Spring Strawberry-Rhubarb Shrub (page 113).

Dressings, Sauces, and Marinades

BASIC APPLE CIDER VINAIGRETTE

This vinaigrette is one of the real workhorses of my kitchen. Delicious and versatile in and of itself, it's also just the right canvas for building other dressings. It is super easy to scale up. You'll probably end up keeping a stash of it in the fridge most of the time for drizzling and dousing onto all manner of things. Like . . . cream cheese and crackers. Yep, really!

Yield: about 1¼ cups vinaigrette

¼ cup apple juice or cider
¼ cup apple cider vinegar
1½ teaspoons kosher salt, or to taste
Freshly ground black pepper
¾ cup extra-virgin olive oil

1. Pour the apple juice and vinegar into a small bowl, add the salt and several generous grinds of black pepper, and stir to dissolve the salt.

2. Slowly whisk in the olive oil, pouring it in a thin, steady stream. Use immediately.

HONEYED APPLE
CIDER VINAIGRETTE

Here, I've taken vinaigrette a step beyond basic, adding honey, garlic, and lemon for balance and depth. The tang of apple cider vinegar along with the hint of sweetness makes this a great dressing for almost any vegetable or salad dish. I make it at least once a week, partly because I find that keeping plenty of dressing on hand helps remind me to eat more salad!

Yield: about 1¼ cups vinaigrette

½ cup honey, preferably raw, organic
¼ cup apple cider vinegar
Juice of 1 lemon
1 garlic clove, minced
¾ cup extra-virgin olive oil
Coarse salt and freshly ground black pepper

In a small bowl, whisk together the honey, vinegar, lemon juice, and garlic. Slowly whisk in the olive oil, pouring it in a thin, steady stream. Season with salt and pepper to taste.

CIDER DIJON DRESSING

This is a classic French vinaigrette. Utter simplicity. If you like, you can substitute whole-grain mustard for the smooth Dijon called for in the recipe. It adds a bit of texture, which is nice in simple salads, such as steamed haricots verts and potatoes or over a mountain of mixed greens.

Yield: about 1 cup dressing

1 tablespoon finely chopped shallot

1 tablespoon Dijon mustard

¼ cup apple cider vinegar

⅔ cup extra-virgin olive oil

Salt and freshly ground black pepper

In a medium bowl, whisk together the shallot, mustard, and vinegar. Slowly whisk in the olive oil, pouring it in a thin, steady stream, then season with salt and pepper to taste.

QUICK MISO PRIMER

Miso is a naturally fermented paste made from cooked soybeans, salt, and often another ingredient, such as white rice, brown rice, or barley. The color can range from light to reddish to chocolate brown, and the flavor can be mildly salty and sweet to strong and very salty. Generally speaking, the darker the color of the miso, the saltier it is. You can keep unopened miso at room temperature indefinitely. Once opened, keep covered in the refrigerator and consume it within a year of purchase.

SESAME MISO VINAIGRETTE

In this delicious dressing, our beloved action hero teams up with miso, a fermented soybean paste, to form a nutritional silver bullet. Miso, like apple cider vinegar, is a living, fermented food, and it contains tons of enzymes, micronutrients, active cultures, and probiotics, all of which support immunity and digestion. It adds a delicious salty pop to the dressing. And, like many fermented foods, which are high in the glutamate proteins (better known as umami or "the fifth taste"), it adds a special savoriness here. The dressing is great on vegetable salads, but don't stop there—grains, noodles, and beans love this stuff, too. Better yet, try it in place of mayo for a fun, Asian spin on chicken or tuna salad.

Yield: about 1 cup vinaigrette

¼ **cup tahini**

1 tablespoon red miso (or another miso of your choice)

1 tablespoon apple cider vinegar

½ **teaspoon sesame oil**

¼ **cup warm water, plus more as needed**

Freshly ground black pepper

In a small bowl, combine the tahini, miso, vinegar, and sesame oil. Stir to form a smooth paste. Whisk in the warm water gradually, adding additional water a tablespoon at a time, if necessary, until the desired consistency is reached. Season with black pepper to taste.

GREEN GODDESS DRESSING

Green goddess dressing has been around for ages. It was created in California in the 1920s and was a salad menu staple for years. While not quite as popular as it once was—maybe having something to do with the fact that both mayonnaise *and* sour cream are among its ingredients, nudging it over the line into overkill territory—I think its creamy, herby tang is so gorgeous that I was determined to give it an update. This healthy version, with creamy Greek yogurt, is delicious over tender lettuces, stirred into chicken salad, or served as a party dip.

Yield: about 1½ cups dressing

2 garlic cloves, minced
1 cup loosely packed fresh basil
⅓ cup loosely packed fresh parsley leaves
½ cup plain Greek yogurt
2 tablespoons apple cider vinegar
2 tablespoons extra-virgin olive oil
Kosher salt

In a medium bowl, whisk together the garlic, basil, parsley, yogurt, and vinegar. Slowly whisk in the olive oil, pouring it in a thin, steady stream, then season with salt to taste.

CHIMICHURRI SAUCE

Chimichurri is an Argentinean condiment that is typically served with grilled meats, although after making it yourself you'll be thinking up zillions of other foods to eat it with. I like to serve it instead of butter with a warm baguette, use it as the dip for crudités, stir it into scrambled eggs, and frost my kids' birthday cakes with it. Well, I would if they'd let me. Instead, I drizzle it on meat.

Yield: about 2 cups sauce

2 cups packed fresh flat-leaf parsley leaves

¼ cup apple cider vinegar

4 medium garlic cloves, smashed

¼ cup packed fresh oregano leaves,
    or 4 teaspoons dried

½ teaspoon red pepper flakes

½ teaspoon kosher salt

Freshly ground black pepper

1 cup extra-virgin olive oil

In a food processor, combine the parsley, vinegar, garlic, oregano, and red pepper flakes. Process until smooth; season with salt and black pepper. Transfer the sauce to a bowl and pour the olive oil over the mixture. Let stand for at least 20 minutes. The chimichurri will keep in the refrigerator for up to 1 week.

APRICOT DRESSING

I live in a household of dried apricot fans. My family can't seem to get enough of these chewy little gems, so we keep our pantry well stocked. They're great on their own, of course, but as it turns out, apricots pair incredibly well with apple cider vinegar, and this dressing is a fantastic marriage of the two. All at once sweet, tangy, and piquant, it's as bright and sunny as a summer day! I particularly like it atop a grain salad with some sort of salty cheese, to balance the sweetness. Try this formula: 1 or more cups cold cooked grains, ½ cup fruit or vegetables, something salty, something crunchy, a handful of chopped herbs and/or something sweet. Dinner. Done.

Yield: about 1½ cups dressing

½ cup apricot nectar

⅓ cup apple cider vinegar

1 tablespoon Dijon mustard

½ teaspoon salt

½ cup extra-virgin olive oil

3 scallions, thinly sliced

½ cup dried apricots, thinly sliced

In a large bowl, whisk together the apricot nectar, vinegar, mustard, and salt. Slowly whisk in the olive oil, pouring it in a thin, steady stream. Once emulsified, stir in the scallions and dried apricots.

CAROLINA-STYLE BBQ SAUCE

When it comes to barbecue in the United States, the sauce is what distinguishes one regional style from another. From Memphis to Kansas City, from the Carolinas to Texas, sauces range from sticky and sweet to mustardy, vinegary, and fiery. I do like all barbecue, but I am partial to the vinegar-based North Carolina 'cue. There, the barbecue is chopped, then dressed with spicy vinegar sauce—a perfect complement to the meat's earthy smoke. While pulled pork is traditional, the sauce is great on chicken, turkey, brisket, mushrooms, you name it. Basically, if it's good on the grill, it'll be good with the sauce.

Yield: about 2½ cups sauce

2 cups apple cider vinegar

3 tablespoons ketchup

2 tablespoons paprika

2 tablespoons dark brown sugar

4 teaspoons kosher salt

1 tablespoon hot sauce

1 teaspoon cayenne pepper

**1 teaspoon freshly ground
    black pepper**

In a glass jar or bottle combine all the ingredients. Mix or shake until the sugar and salt dissolve. Refrigerate for at least 24 hours and up to 6 months.

APPLE CIDER VINEGAR MAYONNAISE

You may be surprised to know that making mayonnaise at home is an incredibly simple undertaking. All you need is a bowl, a whisk, and a few everyday ingredients. The resulting sauce is creamy and rich, with a natural tanginess that beats the pants off the jarred stuff every time. It's great as a sandwich spread, of course, but you'll also love it with simple grilled fish, boiled potatoes, and vegetables, or slathered on crusty bread. Feel free to play with the flavor of your mayo—try adding crushed garlic, curry powder, fresh herbs, or citrus zest. Just make sure all of your ingredients are at room temperature before you get started, or else the sauce will break down.

Yield: about 2 cups mayonnaise

2 large egg yolks
1½ teaspoons Dijon mustard
1 tablespoon apple cider vinegar
2 cups extra-virgin olive oil
Salt and freshly ground black pepper

In a bowl, combine the egg yolks, mustard, and vinegar, and stir with a whisk. Add the olive oil in a slow, steady stream, whisking constantly. Whisk increasingly faster until it takes the thick consistency of mayonnaise. Whisk in salt and pepper to taste.

Food Safety Note: This recipe calls for uncooked eggs. To reduce the risk of foodborne illness, use pasteurized eggs.

HOMEMADE SPICED KETCHUP

Ketchup is one of those things you can find hanging out on the door of most American refrigerators, and mine is no exception. With all manner of oven fries (sweet potato, herbed, Parmesan…) in heavy rotation around here, we go through a lot of ketchup in our house. But, since most store-bought versions contain ingredients I don't love (like high-fructose corn syrup and weird preservatives), I prefer to make my own. It's pretty simple to do with basic ingredients and a blender or food processor. I sweeten mine with brown sugar and molasses and add a variety of spices, resulting in a complex, fresh and bright condiment. Many ketchup recipes call for long simmering times, but since high heat can destroy the beneficial enzymes and nutrients in apple cider vinegar, I just blitz canned tomato paste with the rest of the ingredients in a blender. It's simple to make and just as good!

Yield: about 2½ cups ketchup

12 ounces tomato paste

½ cup dark brown sugar

½ teaspoon mustard powder

½ teaspoon kosher salt

½ scant teaspoon ground cinnamon

2 pinches of ground cloves

2 pinches of ground allspice

1 pinch of cayenne pepper

⅔ cup water

¼ cup apple cider vinegar

1. Using an immersion blender, food processor, or blender, purée all the ingredients until smooth.

2. Adjust the seasonings as needed, and pour the ketchup into a container and seal. The ketchup can be refrigerated for up to 1 month.

CLASSIC GRAINY MUSTARD

Making mustard is easy and, because there are endless variations when adventuring with mustard DIY—it's fun, too. This recipe is for a fairly basic Dijon-style brown mustard with a rustic, grainy texture, which adds a lovely pop to potato salad or on top of sausage. The hardest part about making your own mustard is the waiting—you can't eat it right away, and it's best to wait a couple of days before you really dig in. Rest assured, however, it'll be worth it! Your homemade mustard will be bitter at first. This is normal, and within a couple of days it will start to mellow out. Within a week or two you'll find it will be right where you want it, the kind of mustard dreams are made of. Mustard lasts forever in the fridge, thanks to all that vinegar, so don't hold back if you want to make a double batch and save yourself some time down the road.

Yield: about 1½ cups mustard

½ cup dry white wine, such as sauvignon blanc

½ cup apple cider vinegar

¼ cup brown mustard seeds

¼ cup yellow mustard seeds

½ teaspoon kosher salt

1. In a small, nonreactive bowl, stir all the ingredients until combined. Cover tightly with plastic wrap and let sit at room temperature for 2 days.

2. Remove the plastic wrap and transfer the mustard mixture to a blender or food processor. Purée until the desired consistency is reached, about 30 seconds for a coarse texture, longer for a smoother mustard. Transfer the mustard to a small, nonreactive container, such as a glass jar, with a tight-fitting lid, cover, and refrigerate.

PEACHY HONEY MUSTARD

I used to have a very complicated relationship with peaches. I went through life hoping for the best but expecting the worst from every peach whose path I crossed, which might sound like a euphemism for one's life during her single years in New York City, but I swear I'm actually talking about peaches. It's like this: a perfect peach is fragrant, soft, juicy, sweet, and bright. Poetry on your tongue. Sunshine in your mouth. But because eating a perfect peach can be such a transcendent experience, a less-than-perfect peach—mealy, mushy, and tasteless—is an utter slap in the face. Or so I believed, until I found a place for those less-than-perfect, past-their-prime, bruised, has-been peaches: mustard. Whenever I find a peach in my fruit bowl that's overstayed its welcome, I make this fruity, hot mustard. It's seriously delicious.

Yield: about 1½ cups mustard

¼ cup yellow mustard seeds

2 tablespoons brown mustard seeds

½ cup apple cider vinegar

1 large peach, peeled, pitted, and chopped into chunks

2 tablespoons honey

½ teaspoon garlic powder

¼ teaspoon ground turmeric

¼ teaspoon paprika

¼ teaspoon salt

1. In a small bowl or jar, combine the mustard seeds and vinegar. Cover and refrigerate overnight to soften.

2. Transfer the mustard seed mixture to a blender or food processor. Puree until the desired consistency is reached, about 30 seconds for a coarse texture, longer for a smoother mustard. Add the peach, honey, garlic powder, turmeric, paprika, and salt and blend until evenly incorporated. Taste and adjust the seasoning as necessary.

3. The mustard will keep, refrigerated in a jar or airtight container, for up to 1 month.

HARD CIDER MUSTARD

I live in the Northeast, where fall is a most beautiful season. Each year, I look forward to crisp temperatures, colorful foliage, autumn's bumper crop of squash, sweet potatoes, apples, and pears—and my family's annual pilgrimage to a local u-pick apple farm. Many of the local orchards brew their own hard cider, which my husband and I are most happy to sample at home after learning the hard way that dragging two kids and 6 tons of apples in our Radio Flyer wagon through what feels like miles of endless apple orchards looks really sweet in pictures, but is actually kind of poor planning. Also, because cider brewed from these awesome orchards is very tasty. We usually bring home enough that I have an extra bottle or two to use in braises or—our favorite—this fantastic mustard. It's the perfect way to heat and excite our palate through the chilly fall and frosty winter months.

Yield: about 4 cups mustard

½ cup brown mustard seeds

½ cup yellow mustard seeds

¼ cup yellow mustard powder

1 cup apple cider vinegar

1½ cups hard apple cider

1 tablespoon kosher salt

¼ cup honey

2 Granny Smiths or similarly tart apples, peeled, cored, and finely chopped

1. In a medium glass or ceramic bowl, place the mustard seeds and powder along with the cider vinegar and hard cider. Set aside, covered (but not sealed airtight), for 24 hours.

2. In a food processor, place the soaked mustard mixture along with the salt and honey, and process for 1 to 2 minutes, until the seeds are coarsely ground. Add the chopped apple and pulse a few times to incorporate.

3. The mustard will be very pungent at first. Cover and refrigerate for a few days (or to taste) before using.

CHIPOTLE MUSTARD

This mustard is smoky and fruity from the chipotle chile, and not-kidding-around hot. I love it on grilled chicken, in sandwiches, and even in tacos—but my favorite use for this mustard is for dipping. If you want your mind blown, use it as a dip for homemade pretzels. This mustard is actually cooked quickly with egg and cornstarch to achieve an amazingly silky texture. Crazy delicious.

Yield: about 1 cup mustard

⅓ cup mustard powder

½ cup apple cider vinegar

1 tablespoon minced canned chipotle chile in adobo (removed from sauce)

1 large egg

½ teaspoon salt

2 teaspoons cornstarch

2 tablespoons adobo sauce from chile can

1. In a medium bowl, stir together the mustard powder and vinegar until smooth. Stir in the minced chipotle chile. Chill, covered, overnight.

2. Bring a medium saucepan filled with 1 inch of water to a simmer. Add the egg, salt, and cornstarch to the mustard mixture and whisk to blend. Set the bowl over the simmering water and cook, whisking constantly, until just thickened, 3 to 5 minutes. Stir in the adobo sauce. The mustard will keep, refrigerated in a jar or airtight container, for up to 1 month.

CHUTNEY 4 WAYS

Chutney, made from fruit, sugar, vinegar, and spices, with origins in southeast Asia, is an extremely versatile condiment. Be it mild or hot, smooth or chunky, I love to eat sweet/tart/savory chutney with all manner of curries, of course, but it's also great as an accompaniment to grilled foods, alongside crackers or—my favorite—snuck inside a grilled cheese sandwich. Here are four chutneys that beautifully highlight apple cider vinegar's unique character.

Mango Chutney

Fragrant and sweet, this chutney is a beautiful addition to a cheese platter. Be sure to use ripe mangoes for ultimate sweetness.

Yield: about 3 cups chutney

4 mangoes, peeled, pitted, and chopped

3 tablespoons grated fresh ginger

1 small white onion, chopped

1 garlic clove, minced

½ red bell pepper, seeded and chopped

½ cup golden raisins

⅓ cup sugar

2 teaspoons salt

½ cup apple cider vinegar

⅓ cup water

In a medium saucepan, combine all the ingredients. Over high heat, bring to a boil, then lower the heat to low and simmer until the mangoes are soft and the sauce is thick and syrupy, 45 to 60 minutes. Remove from the heat and allow the chutney to cool. Store in the refrigerator for up to 6 months.

Cranberry Chutney

An obvious choice for jazzing up a holiday table, this chutney pairs beautifully with Thanksgiving turkey. Easily scaled up, it also makes a lovely edible gift.

Yield: about 3½ cups chutney

4 cups fresh or frozen cranberries (about 1 pound)
½ small red onion, minced
1 jalapeño pepper, seeded and minced
1 garlic clove, minced
1 cup packed dark brown sugar
½ cup granulated sugar
1½ cups apple cider vinegar
1 tablespoon minced fresh ginger
1 tablespoon whole mustard seed
1 tablespoon freshly grated
    orange zest
1 tablespoon salt

In a large saucepan, combine all the ingredients and bring to a boil over high heat. Simmer, uncovered, stirring often, until the cranberries have broken down and the mixture has thickened, 10 to 15 minutes. Let cool completely. Transfer the chutney into clean jars and refrigerate. Store in the refrigerator for up to 6 months.

Tomato Chutney

This chutney is the perfect way to preserve summer's tomato bounty. Although considerably less sweet, you can substitute green tomatoes for ripe ones; the resulting condiment is wonderfully tangy.

Yield: about 1½ cups chutney

1¼ cups apple cider vinegar

¾ cup dark brown sugar

1 teaspoon salt

2 teaspoons mustard seeds

½ teaspoon freshly ground black pepper

½ teaspoon red pepper flakes

1 pound ripe tomatoes, diced

1 red bell pepper, seeded and diced

¾ cup chopped scallion greens

In a medium saucepan, combine the vinegar, brown sugar, salt, mustard seeds, black pepper, and red pepper flakes; bring to a boil over high heat, stirring occasionally. Add the tomatoes, bell pepper, and scallions. Simmer the mixture, uncovered, stirring occasionally, for about 1 hour, or until thickened and reduced to about 1½ cups. Let cool completely. Transfer the chutney into clean jars and refrigerate. Store in the refrigerator for up to 6 months.

Rhubarb Chutney

This sweet-and-sour chutney works with almost any meat, but it really comes to life when served alongside goat cheese and crackers. Either fresh or frozen rhubarb works here, so you can chutney (yes, I'm using it as a verb) year-round!

Yield: about 5 cups chutney

4 cups sliced rhubarb

3 cups sliced onion

1 cup raisins

3 cups light brown sugar

2 cups apple cider vinegar

1 tablespoon salt

1 teaspoon ground cinnamon

1 teaspoon ground ginger

½ teaspoon ground cloves

⅛ teaspoon cayenne pepper, or to taste

In a large saucepan, combine all the ingredients and bring to a boil over high heat. Simmer, uncovered, stirring often, until the rhubarb is soft and the sauce is thick and syrupy, 30 to 45 minutes. Remove from the heat and allow the chutney to cool. Store in the refrigerator for up to 6 months.

JERK MARINADE

My husband and I went to Jamaica a few years ago and I have no shame in admitting that some days we ate jerk chicken at more than one meal. We honestly couldn't get enough. Fiery, smoky, and tender, that traditional style of BBQ chicken is irresistible. Part of the allure is the way it's cooked (on long grills with fragrant smoke from both wood and charcoal), but it's the more-flavor-than-you-can-shake-a-stick-at marinade that visits me in my dreams, full of hot chiles and warm spices. I now use it as an all-purpose marinade for meat, fish, and vegetables as well as chicken. Someday I'll get back to Jamaica and eat jerk chicken for breakfast, lunch, and dinner. Until then, I'll keep making my pretty-darn-close homemade marinade.

Yield: about 3 cups marinade

¾ cup packed dark brown sugar

¾ cup sliced scallions

½ cup canola oil or other neutral oil

½ cup ground allspice

¼ cup minced fresh ginger

¼ cup apple cider vinegar

¼ cup freshly squeezed lime juice

¼ cup soy sauce

1 tablespoon dried thyme

1 teaspoon ground cinnamon

1 teaspoon freshly grated nutmeg

½ teaspoon ground cloves

8 garlic cloves, minced

3 Scotch bonnet or habanero chiles,
  stemmed and minced

Kosher salt, to taste

1. In a blender or food processor, combine all the ingredients and blend until well combined. Store in an airtight container in the refrigerator for up to 1 month.

2. When ready to use, toss to coat whatever you're grilling in the jerk marinade. Cover with plastic wrap; chill for at least 6 hours, or overnight.

Safety Note: Because it's not safe to consume marinades used on raw fish or meat, make extra or reserve a bit and set aside before marinating if you plan to baste during cooking or serve extra marinade as a sauce.

SIMPLE GARLIC AND HERB MARINADE

The first year we grew herbs outside our house, I was faced with an "Herbs Gone Wild" kind of gardening situation. With a sage plant so enormous and unstoppable that it started to dwarf our boxwood shrubs and other herbs (basil, oregano, chives, parsley, mint, and rosemary) up the wazoo, I was blind to any recipe that called for less than ½ cup of fresh herbs. Once I'd pesto-ed everything I could think of (by the way, sub in equal parts sage and mint for the basil in your favorite pesto recipe. It's fabulous!), I started making this marinade. It comes together quickly and—best of all—can be made with whatever combination of fresh herbs you have on hand. I massage it onto whole chicken then roast it; the result is moist, flavorful, and tender.

Yield: about 3 cups marinade

6 large garlic cloves, chopped

1 to 2 cups chopped, fresh herbs (such as basil, parsley, cilantro, chives)

1½ tablespoons coarse salt

½ cup freshly squeezed lemon juice

½ cup apple cider vinegar

1½ cups extra-virgin olive oil

Freshly ground black pepper

In a medium bowl, whisk together all the ingredients. Store in an airtight container in the refrigerator for up to 5 days.

GINGER-SESAME MARINADE

This bright, citrusy marinade is extremely versatile—it works well with steak, chicken, fish (salmon, especially), shellfish, vegetables (shiitake mushrooms and sweet potatoes are unbelievable), and . . . ready for this? Pineapple! Please try this. So. Good.

Yield: about 1 cup marinade

1 medium orange, finely grated to yield ½ teaspoon zest, squeezed to yield ⅓ cup juice

¼ cup apple cider vinegar

2 tablespoons Asian sesame oil

2 tablespoons canola oil or another neutral oil

2 tablespoons soy sauce

5 medium garlic cloves, minced

2 tablespoons finely grated fresh ginger

1 tablespoon sriracha or chili garlic sauce

1 tablespoon dark brown sugar or another sweetener, such as pure maple syrup

½ teaspoon kosher salt

In a small bowl, whisk together all the ingredients. Store in the refrigerator in an airtight container for up to 5 days.

TANGY MUSTARD MARINADE

Here's a great way to use some of that DIY mustard you just made! I like the texture of whole-grain mustard, but smooth Dijon style—either homemade or store-bought—works beautifully. With a touch of sweetness from honey, this one is always a hit with my family. I use it to dress up tofu, chicken wings, and all kinds of kebabs. It's a quick last-minute marinade that can be made with ingredients you probably already have on hand.

Yield: about 1 cup marinade

¼ cup whole-grain or Dijon mustard

¼ cup apple cider vinegar

½ cup whole fresh sage, rosemary or thyme leaves, or 2 tablespoons dried

4 garlic cloves, minced

¼ cup extra-virgin olive oil

1 tablespoon honey

Salt and freshly ground black pepper

1. In a small bowl or jar, combine the mustard, vinegar, herbs, garlic, olive oil, and honey. Season with salt and pepper to taste; whisk or shake well.

2. Coat meat, fish, or vegetables and let stand, covered in the refrigerator, for at least 1 hour. Roast, broil, or grill the meat, fish, or vegetables.

BUTTERMILK-DILL MARINADE

Buttermilk is one of my secret kitchen weapons. I use it to make tangy, ranchlike salad dressings, springy pancakes, flaky biscuits, and killer mashed potatoes. But one of my favorite uses for buttermilk is as a marinade for chicken, because while it imparts lovely flavor, the acid in buttermilk also works to seriously tenderize the meat. Like buttah. Although, if you're like most home cooks, you probably don't regularly keep buttermilk in the fridge. (Oh, but you should; the stuff is pure magic, I tell you!) Fear not. If you've got milk and vinegar, you're in business. To make your own buttermilk in a pinch, simply mix 1 tablespoon of apple cider vinegar with 1 cup of milk and let it sit for 5 to 10 minutes. Then go marinate something—such as chicken, fish, or zucchini—with this beauty:

Yield: about 1 cup marinade

½ cup buttermilk

2 tablespoons chopped fresh dill

2 tablespoons apple cider vinegar

1 tablespoon grated lemon zest

3 garlic cloves, chopped (about 2 tablespoons)

1. In a small bowl, whisk together all the ingredients until well combined.

2. Coat chicken, fish, or vegetables and let stand, covered. Marinate chicken for at least 1 hour and up to 24 hours, fish for 15 to 30 minutes, and vegetables for at least 1 hour.

GRILLED ZUCCHINI WITH CHILES, MINT, AND APPLE CIDER VINEGAR

This utterly simple, real looker of a salad's whole is certainly greater than the sum of its parts. I love its gorgeous simplicity, but I have been known to jazz things up even more with toasted nuts, tangy goat cheese, and other adornments. I like to use Thai bird's-eye chiles or red serrano peppers, both for their assertiveness and for the nice hit of color they provide, but feel free to use what appeals to your heat tolerance and taste. If you should happen to end up with leftovers, consider throwing a tangle of this salad on top of a sandwich or as a bed for a lovely piece of grilled fish.

Serves 4 as a side dish

2 to 3 large zucchini, sliced lengthwise
  into ¼-inch-thick strips
1 to 2 tablespoons extra-virgin olive oil,
  plus more for brushing
Salt and freshly ground black pepper

1 fresh red chile, seeded, thinly sliced

1 tablespoon apple cider vinegar

**A handful of fresh mint leaves, roughly
chopped or torn by hand**

1. Preheat a grill or grill pan to high heat.

2. Using a pastry brush, brush the zucchini with olive oil
   on both sides, and season with salt and pepper to taste.
   When the grill is hot, cook the zucchini slices, turning
   once, until well browned, 2 to 3 minutes per side.

3. Arrange the grilled zucchini on a large platter and
   sprinkle evenly with the chile slices and torn mint.
   Drizzle the olive oil and vinegar on top. Serve warm or
   at room temperature.

CREAMY BROCCOLI SLAW

While this recipe calls for shredded broccoli stalks, the use of prepackaged broccoli slaw (made from sweet and crunchy broccoli stems) is a perfectly acceptable shortcut that yields the same cool and refreshing side dish you'd get from shredding your own. Try adding grated carrots or shredded purple cabbage for a colorful twist.

Serves 4 as a side dish

⅓ cup sliced almonds

¾ teaspoon salt, divided

1 cup Greek yogurt

¼ cup buttermilk

3 tablespoons apple cider vinegar

2 tablespoons mayonnaise

2 teaspoons Dijon mustard

¼ teaspoon freshly ground black pepper

5 cups shredded or julienned broccoli stalk (or one 12-ounce bag packaged broccoli slaw)

1. Preheat the oven to 300°F. On a rimmed baking sheet, place the almonds and ¼ teaspoon of the salt, and shake to combine. Toast until aromatic, about 10 minutes. Set aside and allow to cool.

2. In a large bowl, combine the yogurt, buttermilk, vinegar, mayonnaise, mustard, remaining ½ teaspoon of salt, and pepper. Whisk to incorporate.

3. Add the shredded broccoli to the dressing and toss to combine. Sprinkle with the cooled nuts and serve.

PERFECT TOMATO SALAD

This is the salad I want to make almost every day when tomatoes are at their peak in summer. The trick here is to combine tomatoes of different colors and different varieties—such as yellow, orange, green zebra striped, even purple—which makes for a salad that is both beautiful to look at and interesting to eat. And please don't skimp on the salt—it enhances and intensifies the flavor of the tomatoes, making them taste more tomato-y somehow. While this simple salad needs no additional embellishment, who could blame you if you absolutely had to top a thick slice of bread with homemade mayonnaise and a pile of this stuff?!

Serves 4 as a side dish

2 pounds mixed ripe heirloom tomatoes, cored—large ones sliced ¼-inch thick, small ones halved

Sea salt and freshly ground black pepper

2 to 3 tablespoons extra-virgin olive oil

1 tablespoon apple cider vinegar

2 tablespoons minced fresh chives

1 fresh red chile, seeded and chopped

Arrange the tomatoes on a platter. Sprinkle with salt and pepper and drizzle with the olive oil and vinegar. Scatter the chives and chile on top. That's all, folks!

DILL PICKLE POTATO SALAD

I'm always sad to arrive at the end of a jar of pickles, not only because I wish there were more to eat, but also because I kind of hate to part with the tasty brine. This otherwise fairly classic potato salad is a good way to use up some leftover pickle brine, which adds real punch to the finished product. Brine from the Same-Day Cucumber Pickles with Dill (page 104) works especially well here, but you could use the juice from almost any of the recipes in the next chapter or even a jar of store-bought pickles, and still end up with a darn tasty salad.

Serves 4 as a side dish

3 pounds small Yukon gold potatoes
½ cup mayonnaise

¼ cup strained pickle brine

½ small red onion, minced

2 tablespoons chopped fresh dill

2 tablespoons chopped, fresh flat-leaf parsley

Kosher salt and freshly ground black pepper

1. Place the potatoes in a large saucepan of cold salted water. Bring to a boil, then lower the heat and simmer for about 15 minutes, or until a paring knife inserted into them meets no resistance. Drain the potatoes and allow them to cool.

2. Meanwhile, in a large bowl, combine the mayonnaise, pickle brine, red onion, dill, and parsley.

3. Once the potatoes have cooled, break them up by hand into rough chunks, then add them to the dressing and toss to coat. Season with salt and pepper to taste.

Tip: Five more ways to use leftover pickle brine:

1. Make more pickles! Just throw hard-boiled eggs, onions, garlic, even canned beets into a pickleless jar of brine. In a few days you'll have pickles all over again.

2. Use it to marinate and tenderize meat.

3. Liven up store-bought condiments by adding pickle juice by the tablespoonful.

4. Use it in place of vinegar in salad dressings.

5. Add it to your next Bloody Mary or dirty martini.

RAW BEET, FETA, AND QUINOA SALAD

Roasted beets—sweet, earthy, lightly caramelized—are delicious in salads; this we know. But have you tried eating them raw? Sweet and crunchy, they can be julienned, shaved, or grated for a crunchy and sweet variation on a theme. In fact, they're so sweet, that I think they practically beg for a good dose of acid to balance them out. One of my favorite complements to raw beets is the Apricot Dressing (page 38). I especially like it in this salad, because it is acidic enough to stand up to the beets' sweetness, yet sweet enough to balance the saltiness and funkiness of the feta. Use it where called for below, though in a pinch you can certainly use whatever vinaigrette you have on hand. While red beets are readily available in most markets, any color beets will work here and a combination creates a pretty plate. If you've got a spiralizer among your plethora of kitchen gadgets, feel free to noodle up those beets instead of grating them!

Serves 4 as a side dish, 1 to 2 as a main course

½ cup uncooked quinoa, rinsed

½ cup Apricot Dressing (page 38)

1½ pounds beets, peeled and grated

2 tablespoons finely shredded, fresh mint leaves

2 tablespoons finely shredded, fresh flat-leaf parsley

½ cup crumbled feta cheese

Salt and freshly ground black pepper

1. In a medium pot, combine the rinsed quinoa and 1 cup water. Bring the mixture to a boil, then cover, lower the heat to low, and simmer for 15 minutes. Uncover the pot, drain off any excess water, and fluff the quinoa with a fork. Set it aside to cool.

2. In a large bowl, combine the Apricot Dressing, beets, herbs, quinoa, and feta. Toss to combine. Taste and adjust for seasoning.

ASIAN SHREDDED CABBAGE AND CARROT SALAD WITH PEANUTS

This colorful salad is quick, easy, delicious, and a good traveler to boot. The cabbage stays nice and crunchy even hours later, so it makes a nice addition to any potluck spread. I love it as is, but with the addition of tofu, chicken, or even soba or udon noodles it becomes a filling main course salad. (Just be sure to make extra dressing to coat the additional ingredients.) It's also a perfect depository for any bits and pieces or odds and ends you have hanging around the crisper—just toss in whatever's left of the celery, that last sliver of red pepper, and the end of that cucumber you kind of forgot about. The more, the merrier!

Serves 4 as a side dish; serves 2 as a main

3 cups napa cabbage, shredded

4 large carrots, grated

4 scallions, thinly sliced

4 large radishes, thinly sliced

¾ cup Sesame Miso Vinaigrette (page 32)

1 teaspoon sesame seeds, for garnish

¼ cup chopped peanuts, for garnish

In a large bowl, combine the cabbage, carrots, scallions, and radishes. Toss with the dressing. Top with the sesame seeds and peanuts. Serve immediately or chill before serving.

CRAB SALAD WITH APPLES AND CHIVES

This salad makes a fresh and light meal that is reminiscent of lazy summer days. Since fresh lump crabmeat is sold pre-cooked at most fish counters, it's perfect for a fast weeknight dinner. Of course, if you happen to be from Maryland and are a crab-cracking speed demon like my father-in-law (who could probably win a crab picking contest with his eyes closed), by all means start with live crabs—just make sure you end up with about a cup of crabmeat. I like to use the Cider Dijon Dressing (page 31) and recommend you give it a try.

Serves 4 as a starter or side, 2 as a main course

1 pound jumbo lump crabmeat, picked over and drained
2 celery ribs, thinly sliced
1 Granny Smith apple, cored and cut into small dice
2½ tablespoons finely sliced fresh chives, divided
½ cup Cider Dijon Dressing (page 31)
Salt and freshly ground black pepper
1 cup spicy/peppery greens (such as arugula, mustard greens, or watercress)

1. In a large bowl, combine the crabmeat, celery, apple, and 2 tablespoons chives. Add the dressing and gently fold the ingredients together. Taste and add salt and pepper, as needed.

2. To serve: Place the crab salad on a bed of spicy greens and garnish with the remaining ½ tablespoon chives.

WINTRY PANZANELLA WITH SMOKED MOZZARELLA

Panzanella is one of those peasant dishes born of necessity. You see, once upon a time, before monoglycerides, calcium propionate, and calcium sulfate, bread used to get stale, and cooks in countries around the globe came up with clever uses for it. Panzanella is, in my opinion, one of the cleverest of all. Traditionally a summer dish of juicy ripe tomatoes, day-old bread, a few other vegetables, and herbs tossed in a vinaigrette, you wouldn't think it would result in a "wow" meal, but somehow, after a getting-to-know-you period in a big bowl, it does. One particularly long and gloomy winter, while missing the summer weather and—more to the point—summer tomatoes, I decided to find a way to get my panzanella fix (without settling for subpar tomatoes flown in from who knows where?). The following cozy winter vegetable recipe, born of desperation, cured my season-fatigue and gave a home to a halfloaf of bread that was in need of clever repurposing.

Serves 4 to 6

6 cups day-old bread, torn into 1-inch pieces

Extra-virgin olive oil

Salt

1 bunch Tuscan kale, sliced crosswise into ribbons, large stems removed

½ cup red onion, thinly sliced

1 large apple, peeled, cored, and thinly sliced

10 ounces smoked mozzarella cheese, cut into ½-inch cubes

¼ cup toasted and chopped hazelnuts

¼ cup finely chopped fresh sage

¼ cup dried cranberries

½ cup Honeyed Apple Cider Vinaigrette (page 30)

Freshly ground black pepper

1. Preheat the oven to 350°F.

2. In a large bowl, toss the bread pieces with 1 to 2 tablespoons of olive oil and a healthy pinch of salt. Spread them on a sheet pan and place in the oven. Allow the bread to dry out and toast lightly, about 20 minutes.

3. In a large skillet, heat a tablespoon or so of olive oil over medium-high heat. Add the kale and a healthy pinch of salt to the pan, tossing until the kale is just beginning to wilt. Remove from the heat and allow to cool.

4. Place the kale, red onion, apple, smoked mozzarella, hazelnuts, sage, and cranberries in the large bowl with the bread cubes. Add the dressing and toss well to combine. Taste and adjust the seasonings, as necessary. Allow the mixture to sit for at least 30 minutes before serving (this is the hardest part!).

5. Serve at room temperature.

PASTA SALAD: THE NEXT GENERATION

I confess that I kind of like that deli case pasta salad—the one with the sliced black olives, bits of roasted red pepper, and oddly sweet "Italian" dressing. I think it stems from some sort of childhood nostalgia, because for a while, back in the '80s, that kind of thing was all the rage. You'd have been hard-pressed to find a backyard barbecue, buffet table, or salad bar without a shimmering mound of marinating tricolored rotini or tortellini—oh, man, I loved the kind with tortellini. Nowadays, to my chagrin, pasta salad gets a bad rap and I'm not sure why. Sure, a big bowl of cold noodles can be bland, insipid, greasy, underseasoned, and waterlogged. (Yes, deli case, I'm afraid I'm looking back at you.) But it is also quickly assembled, easily transported, endlessly versatile, and a flavorful, fresh, and exciting one-dish meal. Here's a basic (but not boring) formula for a tasty and satisfying pasta salad. Add more vegetables, cured meats, nuts, and/or other herbs to this and you'll accomplish nothing other than making it better and making it your own.

Serves 4 to 6

3 small garlic heads

Extra-virgin olive oil

1 pound short pasta shapes

15 ounces whole or part-skim ricotta

⅓ cup Basic Apple Cider Vinaigrette (page 28)

1¼ teaspoons salt

Freshly ground black pepper

4 (about 1 pound) small tomatoes, roughly diced

1 cup black or green olives, sliced

⅓ cup firmly packed fresh basil leaves, thinly sliced

1. Preheat the oven to 400°F.

2. Slice the top off the garlic heads. Place in the center of a small baking pan and drizzle with olive oil. Cover the garlic tightly with foil and roast for 40 to 50 minutes, or until the garlic is very soft. Remove from the oven and let cool.

3. Meanwhile, cook the pasta in boiling salted water according to the package directions. Drain and place in a large bowl. Toss with a little olive oil, and allow to cool.

4. In a large bowl, whisk the ricotta and Basic Apple Cider Vinaigrette together until lightened and smooth, then squeeze the roasted garlic out of each clove directly into the mixture. Whisk until the garlic is well incorporated. Add the salt and season liberally with pepper.

5. Pour the ricotta mixture over the pasta and add the tomatoes, olives, and basil. Toss to coat. Taste and season further, as needed.

6. Serve chilled or at room temperature.

Flavor Tip: To make sure your pasta salad—or any pasta dish—is well-seasoned and flavorful, don't forget to salt the pasta cooking water. Seasoning the pasta water is the only chance you have to flavor the pasta itself, so it's an important step that shouldn't be neglected.

Pickles

I love pickles, and, as such, have been excited by what seems to be a full-on pickle rage that's happening right now. With an amazing variety of produce and brine landing in jars all over the place, DIY-ers are small-batching the heck out of pickles. Canning and preserving in general is gaining popularity, though I, for one, have tended to shy away from what appears to be an intricate, time-consuming, labor-intensive hobby. Whole weekends of sterilizing and processing and who knows what else goes into "putting up," as they call it? Just. No. But insufficient enthusiasm for canning doesn't stop this sort-of DIY-er from making her own pickles at home. Why? Refrigeration! The pickles in this chapter aren't intended for long-term storage, but they're incredibly easy to make, taste fantastic, and are ready for snacking right out the jar in a relatively short time.

Each recipe involves making a brine and then submerging the items to be pickled in that brine. (That's pretty much all there is to pickling, folks.) In some of the recipes, you'll be instructed to bring all the brine ingredients to a boil in a small pan and then pour the brine over the vegetables. This process makes for good pickles. But since much of apple cider vinegar's magic is gone once the stuff gets heated, I always keep some of a pickle recipe's vinegar off the heat, saving it as an addition at the end. It's kind of a best-of-both-worlds solution.

Refrigerator pickles will keep for about a month. If they develop any funky or weird smells, or if you notice that they've started to effervesce (a sign of fermentation), it's best to just chuck them. Pretty unlikely they'll be hanging around long enough to go bad, though. You'll be amazed how quickly homemade pickles disappear from your fridge!

SPICY PICKLED APRICOTS

Fresh apricots are fabulous on their own, but pickling gives them an intense, tangy-sweet flavor. I especially like them in salad—say, bitter greens, goat cheese, and mint topped with pickled apricots—but add them to fish tacos? Take a bow, maestro.

Yield: 2 pounds pickles

1 cup apple cider vinegar, divided

½ cup sweet vermouth

½ cup honey

½ cup water

2 (3-inch) cinnamon sticks, broken

6 whole cloves

1½ teaspoons red pepper flakes

2 pounds ripe apricots

1. In a medium nonreactive saucepan, combine ½ cup of the vinegar and the vermouth, honey, water, cinnamon, cloves, and red pepper flakes. Bring to a boil, lower the heat to medium-low, and simmer, uncovered, for 5 minutes. Remove from the heat and let stand for 30 minutes. Remove and discard the spices. Stir in the remaining ½ cup of vinegar.

2. Bring a large saucepan of water to a boil. Fill a large bowl with ice water. Carefully lower the apricots into the boiling water and blanch for 30 to 60 seconds. Using a slotted spoon, transfer the apricots from the

boiling water to the ice water. When cool enough to handle, remove the skins.

3. Pit and quarter the apricots. Pack the apricots into clean glass jars, leaving ½ inch of room at the top.

4. Pour the cooled brining liquid over the apricots to cover.

5. Cover and refrigerate at least 24 hours or up to 3 weeks.

PICKLED GREEN BEANS

These hot and sour pickles are a tasty and addictive nibble, especially as part of an antipasto platter or as a side dish at a cookout. But if you're going to take them seriously, I have but two words for you: Bloody. Mary. These pickles stay nicely crisp, even after a fairly long soak in their brine, so they're the perfect edible drink stirrer. If you're planning to serve them to kids, you may want to cut back on the chile. And the vodka. Hehe.

Yield: ¾ pound pickles

¾ pound trimmed green beans

2 cups apple cider vinegar, divided

4 garlic cloves, thinly sliced

2 tablespoons coarse salt

1 tablespoon black peppercorns

2 teaspoons sugar

2 teaspoons red pepper flakes

1. Arrange the green beans and garlic in clean glass jars.

2. In a saucepan, bring 1 cup of the vinegar and the garlic, salt, peppercorns, sugar, and red pepper flakes to a boil. Remove from the heat and allow to cool slightly, then add the remaining cup of vinegar.

3. Carefully pour the mixture into the jars, secure the lids, and let cool to room temperature.

PICKLED COCKTAIL ONIONS

These cocktail onions make a fabulous edible gift, stored in pretty jars and tied with colorful fabric ribbons. I like to tote them along to holiday parties or other occasions where it's nice to have a hostess gift in hand, especially if I know cocktails will be served. In addition to making a lovely drink garnish, they're a great snack, so I always make sure to stockpile a few for my pickle-loving crew at home. When I can find them, I like to include purple pearl onions for a pop of color. To peel the onions, blanch them in boiling water for about 2 minutes, then submerge them in an ice bath; peel (insert muttering of expletives here due to tedium). Or take a shortcut and buy frozen pearl onions—they're not quite as flavorful or crisp as fresh, but they're already peeled and still make for delicious little pickles. I won't tell, I promise.

Yield: 1 pound pickles

¼ teaspoon whole coriander seeds

½ teaspoon peppercorns

2 sprigs fresh thyme

2 cups apple cider vinegar, divided

2 cups water

⅓ cup sugar

1 tablespoon kosher salt

1 pound pearl onions, peeled

½ cup dry white vermouth

1. In a medium saucepan, combine the coriander seeds, peppercorns, thyme, 1 cup of the vinegar, and the water, sugar, and salt. Heat over low heat, stirring, until the salt and sugar dissolve, about 5 minutes.

2. Add the onions. Bring to a boil; allow to boil for just 1 minute, then remove from the heat.

3. Allow to cool to room temperature. Add the vermouth and the remaining cup of vinegar and stir to combine.

4. Transfer the onions and their pickling liquid to a jar. Leave at room temperature for 1 hour, and refrigerate overnight before using.

QUICK PICKLED RED ONIONS

To add a little zing to sandwiches, burgers, and salad, these fast-as-lightning, blushing pickled onions can't be beat. They keep for ages in the fridge, so if you can resist eating them all in one sitting, they'll be at the ready for perking up most anything on your table. Be sure you store the onions in clay, enamel, glass, or stainless steel, since many metals react with the vinegar, altering the flavor and color of the pickles.

Yield: about 1 pound pickles

1 cup apple cider vinegar

1 cup water

2 tablespoons kosher salt

2 tablespoons sugar

¼ teaspoon hot sauce (optional)

2 red onions, thinly sliced

In a small bowl, combine the vinegar with the water. Stir in the salt, sugar, and hot sauce. Add the sliced onions and let sit for at least 1 hour, but ideally overnight.

MEXICAN-STYLE PICKLED VEGETABLES

Mexican-style pickled vegetables, aka escabeche, aka Mexican relish, are like a Mexican version of Italian giardiniera—spicy, briny, and just barely tender. I consider these guys a must with tacos. I have also stuffed them into sandwiches and quesadillas and served them as a side to scrambled eggs and grilled meats; they're good in each way. But, because I can't seem to leave well enough alone when it comes to food, I've also eaten them with pizza—much as you would eat pizza with pepperoncini or a shake of crushed red pepper—and it's pretty fantastic. I can't say they'd be good stirred into your breakfast cereal, but I also can't think of too many meals where these pickles wouldn't make sense.

Yield: about 1 pound pickles

1 bunch large radishes

3 large carrots, peeled

1 kirby cucumber

1 to 2 jalapeño peppers

1 cup loosely packed fresh cilantro leaves

3 cups apple cider vinegar, divided

1 cup water

3 large garlic cloves, smashed

1½ cups sugar

2 teaspoons kosher salt, or more to taste

1. Slice all the vegetables and jalapeño (remove the seeds and membrane from the jalapeños for milder pickles) into rounds or thin slices. In a large bowl, toss the sliced vegetables and cilantro. Set aside.

2. In a medium bowl, combine 2 cups of the vinegar and the water, garlic, sugar, and salt and bring to a boil.

3. Turn off the heat, and let the pan cool until its contents come to room temperature. Remove the garlic. Stir in the remaining cup of vinegar.

4. Transfer the vegetable mixture into clean glass jars. Evenly distribute the pickling liquid among the jars, so that vegetables are covered.

5. Cover and refrigerate for at least 1 day and up to 4 weeks.

PINK PICKLED EGGS

I spent many of my childhood summers at sleepaway camp in Maine. A few times each year, if we were good, the counselors would take our bunk down the road to Roy's Country Store, where we could each pick out a snack or two. It was a big deal. I almost always chose a can of soda and some kind of chocolate, hoping a friend picked a bag of chips or some other salty snack that we could go "splitsies" on. Occasionally, I'd get a gigantic pickle—the supersour kind that came individually packaged. But, despite my intense curiosity, I never got up the nerve to try one of the pickled eggs that sat in the huge jar on the counter near the cash register. I remember it was kind of uncool to like hard-boiled eggs (which, secretly, I did), let alone the specimens that were sitting in murky brine on the dusty counter of that general store that had been around since the beginning of time. So, it wasn't until many years later that I came to discover the delicacy that is a pickled egg. The vinegar cuts the richness of the yolk and transforms the white into something tangy and firm. In this recipe, the addition of beets results in a brilliant fuchsia egg that's a real show-stopper. My kids eat them, which I'm sure has absolutely nothing to do with the fact that I told them they're Magical Fairy Princess Eggs that the cool kids eat.

Yield: 6 pickled eggs

6 hard-boiled eggs, peeled

1 beet, peeled and roughly chopped into 1- to 2-inch pieces, cooked in 1 cup of boiling water for 15–20 minutes

1 cup liquid reserved from beet cooking

1 cup apple cider vinegar, divided

¼ onion, sliced

⅓ cup sugar

3 whole allspice berries

5 whole cloves

1. Place the eggs and cooked beet in a clean glass jar.

2. In a medium saucepan, combine the beet cooking liquid, ½ cup of the vinegar, and the onion, sugar, and spices. Bring to a boil and cook, uncovered, until the sugar has dissolved and the onion is translucent, about 5 minutes. Remove from the heat, add the remaining ½ cup of vinegar, and let cool for a few minutes.

3. Pour the brine over the eggs in the jar, covering them completely.

4. Seal the jar and refrigerate at least 5 days, gently shaking occasionally.

GINGER PEAR PICKLES

When I first started making these pears, I instantly liked them, but I couldn't figure out what exactly they were. Were they a condiment? A dessert topping? A side dish to poultry or pork? I felt like I needed to give myself a "shopping period" like we had at the beginning of the semester in college, when you could try out a whole bunch of classes before finalizing your schedule. It turns out they're a condiment and a dessert topping and a side dish and more. They're equally delicious over a scoop of caramel or vanilla ice cream as they are alongside roast chicken. Plus, the leftover pickling syrup is great stirred into a glass of seltzer or even as part of a cocktail. Letting the pears mellow in the fridge for a month before digging in gives the fruit a chance to soften and the flavors to meld. It'll be hard to resist, but well worth the wait.

Yield: 2 pounds pickles

1 cup apple cider vinegar, divided

2 cups sugar

1 ounce fresh ginger, sliced

1 cinnamon stick

1 teaspoon whole allspice berries

1 teaspoon whole cloves

2 pounds small, firm pears, peeled, cored, and halved

1. In a large pot, combine ½ cup of the vinegar, sugar, ginger, cinnamon, and allspice, and heat over low heat

until the sugar is dissolved, then bring to a boil. Lower the heat to a simmer.

2. Stud each pear with two or three cloves. Add the pears to the pickling syrup and simmer gently for 15 to 25 minutes, until they're barely tender.

3. Remove the pears from the pot and pack into clean glass jars. Return the syrup to a boil for 5 minutes, remove from the heat, and allow to cool for a few minutes. Add the remaining ½ cup of the vinegar, then ladle the syrup over the pears.

4. Seal the jars and refrigerate for 1 month before using.

TURKISH BABY EGGPLANT PICKLES

I visited Turkey years ago and am pretty sure I consumed my body weight in eggplant over the two weeks I was there. I ate it stuffed with grains, with meat, with cheese, with nuts, with other vegetables; I had it fried, grilled, stewed, as a spread, as a soup, and on a sandwich. And once I had an incredible appetizer of pickled eggplant stuffed with walnuts and pomegranate seeds. Tangy and spicy, tender yet crunchy, it's one of the foods I think about when I remember that trip. Here's my attempt to re-create that dish, which makes for lovely party food, served with warm pita bread and assorted Middle Eastern spreads, or as an afternoon snack along with sweet mint tea.

Yield: about 1½ pounds pickles

6 to 8 small baby eggplants
2 teaspoons salt
¼ cup walnuts, minced
¼ cup pomegranate arils (optional)
6 garlic cloves, minced
1 teaspoon aleppo pepper
¼ teaspoon ground allspice
1 tablespoon finely chopped flat-leaf parsley
¼ cup apple cider vinegar
Extra-virgin olive oil

1. Poach the eggplants in boiling, salted water for 5 to 10 minutes, or until they soften slightly. Make a slit lengthwise in each eggplant.

2. In a bowl, mix the salt, walnuts, pomegranate arils, garlic, spices, and parsley. Stuff about a teaspoon of the mixture into each eggplant and place in a jar, stem end up. Pour the vinegar over the eggplants, close the jar, and allow to sit for 12 hours.

3. Discard the liquid at the bottom of the jar. Fill the jar with enough olive oil to cover the eggplants completely. (A ball of aluminum foil or a lid from another jar with weights on top of the eggplants will keep them submerged.)

4. Close the jars, and pickle for 10 to 14 days. Refrigerated, they will keep for 2 weeks once opened.

MAPLE BOURBON CARROT AND PARSNIP PICKLES

Carrots are definitely a staple in our house. They keep well, they taste good, they're portable for snacking, and my kids love them. They roast beautifully for a quick side dish or they crisp up into incredible chips when sliced paper thin, dressed with nothing more than olive oil and salt, then blitzed in a hot oven for a few minutes. But one of my favorite ways to enjoy carrots is to turn them into pickles. Here, they're combined with parsnips for some contrast in both color and flavor (and when rainbow carrots are available at my farmers' market, I snatch them up for this purpose, because they're almost unspeakably beautiful), then they're cured in a sweet and pungent brine that has just a hint of bourbon. I tend to eat these straight out of the jar, but they're a nice snack to serve with drinks or even chopped and added to tuna salad. These pickles are ready to eat after a few hours in the fridge, but they're even better after a few days.

Yield: 1 pound pickles

½ pound carrots, peeled, trimmed to fit your jar, sliced into thin sticks

½ pound parsnips, peeled, trimmed to fit your jar, sliced into thin sticks

1¼ cups cider vinegar, divided

1 cup water

2 tablespoons bourbon

¼ cup pure maple syrup

1 tablespoon salt

1 teaspoon black peppercorns

3 garlic cloves, smashed

1. Over high heat, bring a medium pot of salted water to a boil. Add the carrots and parsnips and blanch for 1 minute, then drain and quickly submerge in a bowl of ice water to stop the cooking.

2. In the same pot, bring ¾ cup of the vinegar, water, bourbon, maple syrup, salt, peppercorns, and garlic to a boil.

3. Once the mixture boils, lower the heat to low and simmer for 2 minutes. Remove from the heat and allow to cool slightly, then stir in the remaining ½ cup of vinegar.

4. Pack the carrots into jars and carefully pour the warm brine over the carrots, making sure the spices are evenly distributed.

5. Let cool to room temperature, then refrigerate. Store in the refrigerator for up to a month.

PICKLED WATERMELON RADISHES

You can certainly use any kind of radish in this recipe, but if you can get your hands on a bunch of watermelon radishes, pale green on the outside, deep fuchsia in the middle, you'll be glad you did. They're sweet, spicy, crunchy, and just so darn pretty! Try them with softened butter and a sprinkling of salt: *très* French. But to transform them into a punchy complement to burgers, sandwiches, and the like, you've got to give pickling a try. A mandoline makes quick work of the slicing here and ensures thin, uniform pickles. If you don't have a mandoline, make sure you use a very sharp knife.

Yield: ¾ pound pickles

1 bunch (about ¾ pound) watermelon radishes, very thinly sliced

1 cup apple cider vinegar, divided

1 tablespoon sugar

1 tablespoon honey

¼ teaspoon peppercorns

¼ teaspoon kosher salt

1 tablespoon freshly squeezed lime juice

2 garlic cloves, roughly chopped

½ jalapeño or other hot pepper, sliced into strips (optional)

1. Wash and dry the radishes, then slice—using a mandoline or sharp knife—to about a ¼-inch thick. Alternatively, you can cut them into matchsticks or wedges.

2. In a medium saucepan over medium heat, combine ½ cup of the vinegar and the sugar, honey, peppercorns, and salt and heat until the sugar is dissolved, about 2 minutes. Remove from the heat. Stir in the remaining ½ cup of vinegar and the lime juice.

3. Place the radishes, garlic, and jalapeño, if using, in a clean jar and pour the pickling liquid into the jar. Cover, let cool, and refrigerate for at least 4 hours. Store in the refrigerator for up to 2 weeks.

QUICK PICKLED APPLES

I haven't always been a fan of having fruit on my dinner plate. When I was a kid, I would hide applesauce, baked apples, Waldorf salad, and fruit compote in my napkin. They were all too sweet and didn't make sense to me as part of a savory meal. While my covert methods may have left something to be desired (though the dog appreciated it), I think my young palate was on to something. I've since come around on the whole fruit-at-dinnertime issue—I love curries, tagines, braises, and stews with fruit. I love grilled fruit alongside grilled meats and the combination of salty cheese and fresh fruit in a salad. I now know that a hit of sweet yet tart fruit—such as these pickled apples—is sometimes just the right accessory to rich or salty foods. Try them piled on top of a pulled chicken sandwich, as part of a cheese tray, or alongside any fried or fatty food that needs a bit of something to cut the richness.

Yield: about 1 pound pickles

2 cups apple cider vinegar, divided

1 cup water

1 cup sugar

2 teaspoons kosher salt

¼ cup peeled and sliced fresh ginger

1 teaspoon whole allspice berries

2 cinnamon sticks

1 teaspoon whole peppercorns

1 pound firm, crisp apples, cored and sliced

1. In a medium saucepan, combine 1 cup of the vinegar and the water, sugar, salt, ginger, allspice, cinnamon sticks, and peppercorns. Bring to a boil and stir to dissolve the sugar.

2. Add the apples, cover, and simmer for 5 minutes, or until they begin to soften.

3. Transfer the apples and their liquid to a bowl and allow to cool completely. Stir in the remaining cup of vinegar and transfer to a clean glass jar with a lid.

4. Refrigerate at least 8 hours and up to 1 month.

SAME-DAY CUCUMBER PICKLES WITH DILL

This is the easiest, quickest pickle recipe you'll ever find. Salt, vinegar, cucumbers, and dill (plus garlic and other spices, if you want to be all fancy about it) get piled into a jar, the jar gets refrigerated for an hour (longer, if you have the time), then— BOOM—pickles. Just like that. My pickle-fiend kids love these, so I usually double the recipe.

Yield: about 2 pounds pickles

8 to 10 kirby cucumbers, very thinly sliced

3 teaspoons kosher salt

1 to 2 tablespoons chopped fresh dill

½ cup apple cider vinegar

1. Place the cucumbers in clean glass jars.

2. In a bowl, combine the salt, dill, and vinegar. Pour the mixture evenly over the cucumbers.

3. Close the jars, shake to distribute the ingredients, then refrigerate for at least 1 hour, but ideally 4 to 6 hours.

APPLE CIDER VINEGAR HEALTH DRINK

This is a lovely and refreshing way to get your daily dose of apple cider vinegar. It's nicer than drinking plain apple cider vinegar—let's be honest—and it takes only a few minutes to make, so you can still get all the health benefits, even on your busiest morning. Sometimes I like to make it with warm water and sip it like tea, though in the chaos of weekday mornings, I usually down it over ice. It's good either way.

Yield: 1 serving

1½ **cups cold filtered water**

2 **tablespoons apple or grape juice**

2 **tablespoons raw apple cider vinegar**

½ **teaspoon ground cinnamon**

½ **teaspoon powdered stevia, or 1 tablespoon honey or
   sweetener of your choice**

Place all the ingredients in a glass and stir to combine.

SPARKLING HONEY ADE

Sparkling water, apple cider vinegar, fresh-squeezed juice, and honey syrup make this honey ade the perfect summer sipper. The recipe is incredibly versatile and can be tweaked a zillion ways to suit your taste and what you've got in stock. I like to infuse the honey syrup with herbs (simply steep about a tablespoon of chopped fresh herbs in the warm honey syrup for half an hour or so, then strain and discard the herbs) and vary the juice. Some of my favorite combinations: lemon and lavender; lime and mint; grapefruit and rosemary. Prepare the honey syrup ahead of time and store in the refrigerator for up to a week.

Serves 2 to 4

2 cups water
1 cup honey
2 to 3 cups sparkling water
¼ cup apple cider vinegar
¾ cup freshly squeezed citrus juice
Ice, to serve (optional)

1. In a saucepan, combine the water and honey over medium heat and bring to a low boil.

2. Remove from the heat and allow to cool. Store in the refrigerator until ready to use.

3. In a glass pitcher, combine the syrup, sparkling water, vinegar, and juice. Stir to combine. Pour into glasses over ice or refrigerate until ready to drink.

GINGER-MOLASSES ELIXIR

This recipe is a riff on an old-school drink called switchel, also known as switzel, swizzle, or Haymaker's Punch, an apple cider vinegar, water, and ginger-based drink dating back to colonial times. It was the thirst-quencher of choice for many hay-harvesting farmers, who would take their Haymaker's Punch into the fields in mason jars and down the stuff like Gatorade. My version calls for the specific combination of molasses and ginger, because that's what I like, but maple syrup, honey, and sugar are more or less interchangeable sweeteners in this instance, so use what you have on hand. Try it sparkling or still, as a cocktail or a soft drink, warm or iced. My husband, a great lover of the Dark and Stormy, happily downs this tasty libation spiked with rum and fizzed with seltzer at cocktail hour. And because I'm a good date, I rarely let him drink alone.

Yield: 1 serving

2 tablespoons apple cider vinegar

4 teaspoons molasses

1 teaspoon grated fresh ginger

1 cup still or sparkling water

Ice or seltzer, to serve (optional)

1. Combine all the ingredients in a jar or glass. Cover and refrigerate at least 2 hours, ideally overnight.

2. Prior to serving, shake or stir well. Pour over ice or mix with seltzer, if desired.

FIRE CIDER

I hope you're ready to have your mind blown, because it's about to happen. Meet fire cider, a traditional folk recipe that combines horseradish, garlic, onion, ginger, hot peppers, citrus, spices, and honey infused in vinegar. What's that? Sounds intense? It's delicious. Really. I know, you're thinking, "She's been sniffing the apple cider vinegar for too long now and she's completely lost her mind." You've got to trust me. This stuff is incredibly delicious *and* really good for you! Concocted with all sorts of antibacterial, antifungal, and antiviral ingredients, this tonic has been used through the ages to prevent colds, clear sinuses, support immunity, aid digestion, boost energy, and increase circulation. It's warming, sweet, spicy, and brazen. You can stir it into water, juice, or tea; add it to soups and dressings; or drink it straight, tough guy–style, like I do in winter. Grrrrr!

Yield: about 5 cups fire cider

½ cup (a little less than ⅓ pound) peeled and diced horseradish

½ cup (40 cloves or 4 heads) crushed garlic

½ onion (about ½ cup), minced

¼ cup (approximately 4 inches) minced fresh ginger

¼ cup (approximately 4 inches) minced fresh turmeric, or 1 tablespoon ground

1 habanero chile, halved

1 orange, zested and juiced

1 lemon, zested and juiced

1 rosemary sprig

1 thyme sprig

1 teaspoon black peppercorns

2 to 3 cups apple cider vinegar

¼ cup raw honey, or more to taste

1. Place all the ingredients, except the honey and vinegar, in a quart-size jar. Fill the jar with the vinegar, covering all the ingredients and making sure there are no air bubbles. Cap the jar. If using a metal lid, place a piece of parchment or waxed paper between the jar and the lid, to prevent corrosion from the vinegar. Shake well. Let the jar sit for 3 to 6 weeks, shaking daily (or as often as you remember).

2. Strain the vinegar into a clean jar. Add honey to taste. Refrigerate and use within a year.

Note: Fresh turmeric is available in the produce section of well-stocked grocery stores, health food stores, and Asian and Indian markets.

HOMEMADE SPORTS DRINK

On the playground, on the soccer field, or at the gym, this drink quickly quenches thirst and replenishes electrolytes for movers and shakers of all sizes. Most commercial sports beverages contain such ingredients as sucrose syrup, glucose-fructose syrup, vague and mysterious "natural flavors," and artificial dyes—not exactly what I want to give my kids or put in my body after working hard to get in shape. This recipe includes the classic combination of lime and coconut, which not only tastes great, but it gives you the perfect excuse to (cue music), "Put the lime in the coconut and drink them both down."

Serves 2 to 4

3 cups coconut water

1 cup water

¼ cup freshly squeezed lime juice

¼ cup apple cider vinegar

¼ teaspoon Celtic sea salt or Real Salt

2 tablespoons raw honey or pure maple syrup

In a pitcher or sports bottles, mix all the ingredients together. Refrigerate until ready to use. Drink within a week.

A SHRUB FOR EVERY SEASON

Chances are, when you hear the word *shrub*, what first comes to mind is not a tangy, refreshing vinegar-based beverage. But a shrub, also known as drinking vinegar, is in fact delicious fruit-infused vinegar syrup that, when added to sparkling water or cocktails, stimulates the appetite, quenches the thirst, and provides quick and energizing refreshment. Shrubs have been around for centuries, dating back to colonial times and earlier, and came to be largely as a way to preserve fruit prior to refrigeration. While they may be old-fashioned, shrubs are kind of a thing right now. They're popular with wellness enthusiasts, who know about the incredible health benefits of apple cider vinegar. And mixologists (that's hipster-speak for "bartenders") are embracing shrubs like crazy, too, because of the magic and complexity that result when fruit, sugar, vinegar, and, in some instances, add-ins, such as herbs and spices, are allowed to mellow and mingle for a bit in the fridge. So, you're going to want to give them a try, if not simply because they're delicious and good for you, but because shrubs will, clearly, help you win friends and influence people. Here are four recipes to try, one for each season.

Spring Strawberry-Rhubarb Shrub

Yield: about 6 cups shrub

1¼ cups ripe strawberries, cleaned, hulled, and sliced

¾ cup rhubarb, wiped clean and sliced

10 black peppercorns, slightly crushed

1½ cups sugar

1½ cups apple cider vinegar

1. In a bowl or jar, combine the fruit, peppercorns, and sugar, stirring to evenly coat the fruit.

2. Cover and refrigerate for 24 hours.

3. Using a wooden spoon or muddler, crush the fruit as much as possible, then return the mixture to the refrigerator for another 24 hours.

4. Using a fine-mesh sieve, strain the liquid from the pulp, and transfer the liquid to a clean glass jar. Add the vinegar and stir well.

5. The shrub will be ready to drink in 1 week and keeps for up to 6 months in the refrigerator.

Summer Raspberry-Peach Shrub

Yield: about 5 cups shrub

1 cup fresh peaches, peeled, pitted, and chopped

1 cup raspberries

1 cup sugar

2 cups apple cider vinegar

1. In a bowl or jar, combine the peaches, raspberries, and sugar, stirring or shaking to evenly coat the fruit.

2. Cover tightly and refrigerate for 24 hours.

3. Give the mixture a gentle press with a wooden spoon or muddler, then using a fine-mesh sieve, strain the liquid from the pulp, and transfer the liquid to a clean glass jar.

4. Add the vinegar to the syrup. Seal the jar and give it a good shake.

5. The shrub will be ready to drink in 1 week and keeps for up to 6 months in the refrigerator.

Autumn Cinnamon-Apple Shrub

Yield: about 4 cups shrub

3 medium apples, cored and grated

1 cup apple cider vinegar

½ cup sugar

2 cinnamon sticks

1. In a bowl, combine the grated apples, vinegar, sugar, and cinnamon, stirring or shaking to evenly coat the fruit.

2. Cover tightly and refrigerate for 24 to 48 hours.

3. Give the mixture a gentle press with a wooden spoon or muddler, then using a fine-mesh sieve, strain the liquid from the pulp, and transfer the liquid to a clean glass jar.

4. The shrub will be ready to drink in 1 week and keeps for up to 6 months in the refrigerator.

Winter Cranberry-Orange Shrub

Yield: about 4 cups shrub

2 cups cranberries

2 tablespoons orange zest

1½ cups sugar

1 cup apple cider vinegar

1. In a bowl or jar, combine the cranberries, orange zest, and sugar, stirring or shaking to evenly coat the fruit. Muddle the mixture to break up the cranberries a bit.

2. Cover tightly and refrigerate for 24 to 48 hours.

3. Give the mixture a gentle press with a wooden spoon or muddler, then using a fine-mesh sieve, strain the liquid from the pulp, and transfer the liquid to a clean glass jar.

4. Add the vinegar, cover, and refrigerate.

5. The shrub will be ready to drink in 1 week and keeps for up to 6 months in the refrigerator.

RISE AND SHINE STRAWBERRY SMOOTHIE

Smoothies are such a lovely way to start the day. They are surprisingly filling and, because they're so quick and easy to make, they fit perfectly into weekday mornings. But have you danced the tragic smoothie dance? It's the one that goes like this: (1) deposit way too many "healthy" ingredients in a blender; (2) with great anticipation and excitement, press a whole bunch of buttons on the machine; (3) watch as nothing actually happens to the ingredients, despite loud whirring noise coming from inside the blender; (4) turn the damn thing off and try stirring the ingredients with a spoon and/or adding more liquid to achieve smoothie-ness; (5) tinker with the ingredients some more, blending on and off, until you end up with a mostly disappointing, too-slushy beverage; (6) drink

it anyway, because it's not like you're going to throw it away after all that. Hrmph.

I've finally figured out a good smoothie formula and I feel like I've cracked a complex code that could dismantle a bomb and save humanity from evil! You want your smoothie to be creamy, cold, nutritious, and filling. So, try to keep this formula in mind when concocting your next one: 1 banana or 1 cup of fruit + ¾ cup of liquid + 1 or 2 tablespoons of healthy fat (nut butter, avocado, whole seeds) + 1 handful of greens + a sweetener (optional) + 1 cup of ice. And don't forget to add a teaspoon or two of apple cider vinegar for brightness and your daily dose of awesomeness.

Serves 1

¾ cup coconut water

2 teaspoons apple cider vinegar

1 cup hulled fresh or frozen strawberries

1 heaping tablespoon almond butter

1 handful fresh spinach leaves

1 cup ice

1. Place the coconut water and vinegar in a blender, then the berries, almond butter, and spinach. Blend until smooth.

2. Add the ice to the blender and blend again until smooth.

3. Drink immediately, ideally with a fun-colored crazy straw, no matter how old you are.

GREEN TEA AND APPLE CIDER VINEGAR TONIC

Green tea is well known for its antioxidant properties and myriad other health benefits. Studies link it to improvements in memory, metabolism, brain health, and cancer defense. It's good for your heart, may help prevent strokes, and can lower your risk for type 2 diabetes. I'm in for all that, so I used to try to break my coffee habit a few mornings a week and drink a cup or two. But I found that, on its own, it was too grassy and bitter for my taste. I just didn't enjoy drinking it. Oh, but it's SO GOOD FOR YOU! What could I do? Thankfully, I found a way around my aversion with this lovely, refreshing tonic. It brings together all the benefits of green tea and apple cider vinegar, which is essentially like drinking a bulletproof vest, and it tastes great. A win-win.

Serves 4 to 6

6 cups water

¼ cup peeled and roughly chopped fresh ginger

3 to 6 green tea bags

½ cup mint leaves

⅓ cup honey

2 tablespoons apple cider vinegar

1. In a medium pot, combine the water and ginger. Bring to a boil, then remove from the heat and add the tea

bags and mint leaves. Cover and steep for about
15 minutes.

2. Using a fine-mesh sieve, strain out the ginger, tea, and
    mint and discard. Add the honey and vinegar to the
    tea and stir to combine.

3. Transfer to a pitcher and let cool to room temperature
    before refrigerating.

SPICED BERRY WARMER

As soon as the weather turns autumnal, I start dreaming about sipping a mug of something warm and spiced on chilly evenings. Mulled cider is a favorite in our house for kids and grown-ups alike. There's something soul-warming about it. For parties, I like to make a more adult version, either spiked with rum or using hard cider in place of regular apple cider—it's a crowd-pleaser! But for something delicious yet out of the ordinary, I make a sweet and tangy berry-infused version that is all at once soothing and invigorating. Try it the next time you come in from a chilly day of raking leaves or playing in the snow.

Serves 4

1 (10-ounce) package frozen, unsweetened raspberries

2 cups cranberry juice (cocktail)

4 cups apple cider

Zest of 1 orange, cut in large strips

1 (1-inch) piece ginger, peeled and sliced

2 (3-inch) cinnamon sticks

4 whole allspice berries

4 whole cloves

¼ cup apple cider vinegar

¼ cup sugar, honey, or sweetener of your choice

In a large pot, place all the ingredients and bring to a boil. Lower the heat and simmer, partially covered, for 30 minutes. Strain and serve warm.

Baked and Griddle Treats

OVERNIGHT WAFFLES WITH WARM APPLE CIDER SYRUP

Once upon a time—before kids—our weekend mornings were relaxing, lazy even. I have vague but pleasant memories of sleeping in, occasionally bingeing on reality TV, leisurely running errands, and enjoying delicious, eggy, waffly brunches. While I've 100 percent happily traded in those slow and easy weekend mornings for six a.m. snuggles and dress-up dance parties with my little girls, I find it a little easier to greet that early start with a smile if I know there's a yummy reward waiting in the kitchen for all of us. These yeast-risen homemade waffles, hot off the iron—crisp on the outside, light and airy inside—are a favorite in our house. The recipe calls for mixing up the batter the night before, so morning prep is lightning fast. And that's a good thing, since I know two little girls who go from sleeping to starving in about 45 seconds flat! The syrup—which will knock your socks off—can also be made ahead of time and rewarmed in the microwave.

Serves 4 to 6

FOR THE WAFFLES:

2 cups milk

2 tablespoons apple cider vinegar

2½ teaspoons active dry yeast

½ cup warm water (100°–110°F)

½ cup (1 stick or 4 ounces) unsalted butter, melted
   and cooled

2 tablespoons sugar

2 large eggs

2 cups all-purpose flour

½ teaspoon salt

¼ teaspoon baking soda

FOR THE SYRUP:

1 cup packed dark brown sugar

2 tablespoons cornstarch

1 teaspoon ground cinnamon

¼ teaspoon ground allspice

¼ teaspoon ground ginger

⅛ teaspoon ground cloves

⅛ teaspoon salt

2 cups apple cider

1½ tablespoons apple cider vinegar

¼ cup (½ stick) salted butter, diced

1. Make the waffles: In a small bowl, combine the milk and vinegar. Set aside for 5 minutes to sour and curdle.

2. In a large bowl, sprinkle the yeast over the warm water. Allow to stand for 5 minutes, until it begins to bubble and "bloom."

3. In the large bowl with the yeast, whisk in the milk mixture, melted butter, sugar, and eggs until well combined. Then add the flour and salt, continuing to whisk until the batter is smooth.

4. Cover the bowl with plastic wrap and refrigerate overnight (8 to 12 hours).

5. The next morning, stir in the baking soda, and whisk vigorously until thoroughly combined. Allow the batter to stand for 5 minutes.

6. As you preheat your waffle maker, make the syrup: In a medium saucepan, stir the brown sugar, cornstarch, cinnamon, allspice, ginger, cloves, and salt until well combined.

7. Stir in the apple cider and vinegar and set the mixture over medium-high heat. Bring to a boil and, stirring constantly, cook for about a minute and a half. Remove from the heat, stir in the butter, and allow the syrup to cool until warm.

8. Cook the waffles according to your waffle maker's instructions, about 5 minutes, until golden brown. Serve immediately, with Warm Apple Cider Syrup.

JOHNNYCAKES WITH WARM APPLE CIDER SYRUP

Breakfast for dinner is a pretty regular occurrence in our house. The kids love it and, since I can almost always pull breakfast together with what I have on hand—even when I should've gone grocery shopping two days ago—egg sandwiches, breakfast burritos, waffles, and pancakes have come to my rescue more than once. Sometimes I plan breakfast for dinner just because my crew loves it so much and we rarely have time to make pancakes and the like on busy weekday mornings. These johnnycakes—cornmeal pancakes, essentially—are delicate yet hearty (with just a touch of sugar), so you can still have fun drizzling them with Warm Apple Cider Syrup (pages 128–29) or maple syrup.

Serves 4

1 cup milk

1 tablespoon apple cider vinegar

1 cup cornmeal

1 teaspoon baking powder

¾ teaspoon salt

2 tablespoons sugar

1 egg

2 tablespoons unsalted butter, melted

2 tablespoons canola oil

**Warm Apple Cider Syrup (pages 128–29) or
    pure maple syrup**

1. In a small bowl, combine the milk and vinegar. Set aside for 5 minutes.

2. Meanwhile, in a large bowl, combine the cornmeal, baking powder, salt, and sugar. Add the egg, milk mixture, and butter and whisk to combine.

3. Heat 1 tablespoon of the canola oil in a large skillet or on a griddle. Pour the batter onto the pan into 2-inch circles, about 2 tablespoons each. Cook until golden underneath, 1 to 2 minutes. Flip the johnnycakes and cook until golden underneath, 1 to 2 minutes more. Serve immediately with Warm Apple Cider Syrup or maple syrup.

BAKED APPLE CIDER DOUGHNUTS (OR DOUGHNUT HOLES OR MINI MUFFINS)

Traditional apple cider doughnuts are a fall ritual in the northeast. They're cake-style doughnuts and they get their distinct flavor from cinnamon, nutmeg, and apple cider used in the batter. They have a crisp exterior and a light interior, and are faintly spiced . . . delicious. (I'm not a comic book expert, but I believe they are my kryptonite.) Alas, they are deep-fried and, much as I would like to eat them every day, I can't pretend not to know a thing or two about nutrition, so I get my fill each fall when we visit our local apple orchards. Then I have to wait during the other three seasons on the calendar. There's a happy ending to this tale, however. The following recipe turns out doughnuts that very closely approximate the real deal. They're tender, tangy, and have a similar flavor without the messy, time-intensive, calorie-leaden frying, so I can get my fix more often. If you don't own a doughnut pan, fear not: you can make "doughnut holes" in a mini muffin pan.

Yield: about 36 doughnut holes/mini muffins
or 16 doughnuts

½ cup milk
1½ teaspoons apple cider vinegar
2 cups apple cider
2 whole cloves
Nonstick cooking spray
2 cups all-purpose flour

1½ teaspoons baking powder

1½ teaspoons baking soda

1 teaspoon ground cinnamon

⅛ teaspoon freshly grated nutmeg

¼ teaspoon salt

1 large egg

2 tablespoons salted butter, melted

⅔ cup light brown sugar

2 tablespoons naturally sweetened applesauce
(no sugar added)

1 teaspoon pure vanilla extract

FOR THE CINNAMON SUGAR COATING:

3 tablespoons unsalted butter, melted

½ cup sugar

1 tablespoon ground cinnamon

1. In a small bowl, combine the milk and vinegar. Set aside.

2. Preheat the oven to 350°F. Spray a mini muffin pan or a doughnut pan with nonstick cooking spray and set aside.

3. In a small saucepan, combine the apple cider and whole cloves. Bring to a boil over medium-high heat, then lower the heat to medium and boil vigorously for 15 to 20 minutes, until reduced to about ½ cup. Remove the cloves from the reduction and allow it to cool to room temperature.

4. In a large bowl, combine the flour, baking powder, baking soda, cinnamon, nutmeg, and salt.

5. In another bowl, whisk the egg, melted butter, and brown sugar until thoroughly combined. Add the applesauce, vanilla, milk-vinegar mixture, and apple cider reduction.

6. Add the wet ingredients to the dry and whisk until the dough is smooth and well combined; do not overmix.

7. Divide the batter among the prepared muffin cups or doughnut wells. Bake until the muffins or doughnuts are firm to the touch and a toothpick inserted in the center of one comes out clean, 9 to 12 minutes.

8. When the doughnuts are cool enough to handle, prepare the cinnamon sugar coating: In a medium bowl, combine the sugar and cinnamon. Dip the tops of each muffin or doughnut into the melted butter, then coat with the cinnamon sugar mixture.

EGGLESS CHOCOLATE BUNDT CAKE (AKA CRAZY CAKE)

The legend goes that Crazy Cake (aka Wacky Cake or Depression Cake) became popular during World War II when homemakers needed to find a way to bake without breaking into their rations (such as eggs, milk, and butter). Instead, they used oil, vinegar, and water to turn out a moist, chocolaty cake that—oh, by the way—is just about as dead-easy as making a cake from a mix and—oh, by the way—is vegan and—oh, by the way—is probably the most delicious science experiment you'll ever conduct in your kitchen (remember vinegar + baking soda = mesmerizing bubbles?). Sprinkle the finished product with powdered sugar or frost with your favorite buttercream. Nothing crazy about that!

Serves 8

Softened butter for pan

3 cups all-purpose flour, plus more for dusting

⅔ cup unsweetened cocoa powder

2 cups sugar

2 teaspoons baking soda

2 teaspoons salt

1 cup vegetable oil

2 cups water

2 teaspoons pure vanilla extract, or 1 teaspoon almond extract

2 tablespoons apple cider vinegar

1. Preheat the oven to 350°F.

2. Grease (generously!) with softened butter and flour a 9-inch Bundt pan.

3. In a large bowl, whisk together flour, cocoa powder, sugar, baking soda, and salt. Pour in the water, vegetable oil, vanilla, and vinegar, whisking thoroughly but quickly, until smooth.

4. Pour the batter into the prepared pan and bake for 45 to 50 minutes, until a tester comes out clean and the cake springs back when gently pressed.

5. Allow to cool in the pan for 10 minutes, then turn out onto a wire rack to cool completely.

APPLE CIDER VINEGAR OATMEAL COOKIES

I love a good oatmeal cookie, but so often, especially when they're supposedly "healthier" (i.e., the recipe calls for some kind of whole-grain flour), they're about as light and tender as a hockey puck. I've found that calling in our old pal apple cider vinegar to react with leavening agents—in this case the baking soda—makes baked goods better, lighter, a balance that is often disturbed when a cookie recipe calls for anything other than white flour. Feel free to change the add-ins. Any nut, chip, or dried fruit works here—even pretzel pieces! Gotta try it to believe it.

Yield: about 24 large cookies

¾ cup (1½ sticks or 6 ounces)
   unsalted butter or coconut
   oil, melted

1¼ cups dark brown sugar

2 tablespoons molasses

1 tablespoon apple cider
   vinegar

1 tablespoon pure vanilla
   extract

1 large egg, lightly beaten

1 cup whole-wheat flour

½ cup unbleached
   all-purpose flour

¾ teaspoon baking soda

½ teaspoon baking powder

½ teaspoon salt

2 teaspoons ground cinnamon

1 cup rolled oats

1½ cups chocolate chips or nuts (or a combination)

1½ cups raisins, dried cherries, or other dried fruit of
your choice

1. Preheat the oven to 350°F. Line two large baking
   sheets with parchment paper.

2. In a large bowl, mix the melted butter, brown sugar,
   molasses, vinegar, and vanilla. Add the beaten egg and
   stir to combine.

3. In a separate bowl, whisk together the flours, baking
   soda, baking powder, salt, and cinnamon.

4. Add the dry ingredients to the wet, mixing until incorporated. Stir in the oats, chocolate chips, and raisins.

5. Use ¼ cup of batter per cookie and space them about
   2 inches apart on the prepared baking sheets. Flat-
   ten the cookies with wet fingers to about a ½-inch
   thickness.

6. Bake for 12 to 15 minutes, until golden around the
   edges but still soft and slightly underdone in the
   centers.

7. Remove from the oven and allow the cookies to cool
   for a few minutes on the baking sheets before trans-
   ferring them to a wire rack to cool completely.

BEAUTY AND GROOMING

SIMPLE HAIR CLEANSE

Ever notice how the shampoo you love, your tried-and-true, seems to stop working after a while? The likely culprit is buildup left from styling products and that very shampoo you've been using forevah, which can weigh hair down and cause dullness. I used to switch brands whenever I thought my shampoo had pooped out on me and even bought pricey clarifying shampoo once or twice when I felt like I was in need of a deep clean. But, as it turns out, apple cider vinegar is kind of magic when it comes to hair. Not only can it help remove buildup, it also works as a natural detangler and general revitalizer. Twice a month, after shampooing, I use an apple cider vinegar rinse and end up with hair that's softer, smoother and super shiny. Here's how to revive your hair:

1 cup apple cider vinegar

1 cup water

1. Combine the vinegar and water in a plastic squeeze
    bottle, empty shampoo bottle, or spray bottle.

2. After shampooing, pour or spray the mixture into
    your hair, then massage it into your scalp. Allow the
    cleanser to sit for a few minutes before rinsing thor-
    oughly with water.

REFRESHING FACIAL TONER

For years, I was diligent with cleansing and moisturizing,
but I was never really sold on toner. I used it on and off over
the years, mostly because it seems to be common knowledge
that people are just supposed to perfume, cleanse, tone, mois-
turize, exfoliate, brighten, lighten, and tighten pretty much
everything from head to toe. Am I right? But the truth is that I
never really noticed any difference in my skin whether or not
it was part of my routine. That is, until I started using apple
cider vinegar on my face. It does something to skin that expensive lotions, fancy cleansers, and—yes, even pricey—toners
don't. Its natural alpha-hydroxy acids and acetic acid shrink
pores, tighten skin, help alleviate acne, and prevent future out-
breaks. It's antibacterial and antiseptic, and it helps balance
your skin's pH. I have yet to find a toner out there that can per-
form this kind of magic. Here's all you need to know:

½ cup apple cider vinegar

1 cup water (filtered or distilled, if possible)

1. Mix together the vinegar and water in a glass bottle, jar, or container.

2. Shake to combine.

3. Moisten a cotton ball or pad, and swipe the mixture over a clean, dry face, avoiding the eye area. Allow the toner to dry (the smell will dissipate quickly).

4. Follow with moisturizer and sunscreen, as usual.

Note: If you have a history of sensitive skin, you may want to start with a gentler solution of ¼ cup of apple cider vinegar and 1 cup of water. Finding the right ratio may require some trial and error, but your glowing skin will thank you for it!

TAKE YOUR TONER TO THE NEXT LEVEL

You can infuse your apple cider vinegar facial toner with fresh herbs, for added nourishment and aromatherapy. Simply simmer a handful of your favorite herbs or even fragrant flower petals (think rose, jasmine, or lavender) in a small saucepan of water over low heat for 30 minutes, strain the mixture through a mesh sieve, allow the infusion to cool, and then use in place of water above.

ALL-NATURAL DEODORANT

Ask me what I think about body odor and I'll tell you it's the pits! (*Ba-dum* crash.) But seriously, folks, throw your commercial deodorant in the trash. Schmearing on stuff that is designed to clog your underarm pores is a routine worth rethinking. For one thing, sweating is good for you! It releases toxins and helps regulate body temperature. Furthermore, your skin is your largest organ and it's very good at absorbing what you put on it. Deodorant is loaded with chemicals, heavy metals, and toxins that easily penetrate the skin and, ultimately, seep into your bloodstream. Such substances as parabens (which have been linked to breast cancer), aluminum (which has been associated with the development of Alzheimer's disease), artificial fragrances, petrochemicals, and other known skin irritants and carcinogens are among the reasons you should consider steering clear of store-bought deodorant. To keep your pits smelling fresh without putting your health at risk, try this:

½ cup apple cider vinegar
½ cup water

1. Mix the vinegar and water in a small bottle or jar. Shake to combine.

2. Use a cotton ball, pad, or soft cloth to apply it under your arms. Allow the mixture to dry. For even easier application, fill an old roll-on deodorant bottle with your all-natural deodorant mixture.

SUNBURN SOOTHER

You slathered on sunscreen, camped out in the shade, and even remembered your hat, but you still managed to slow cook your skin like a roast chicken. Ouch. Of course, your natural instinct is to immediately apply acid to that burning pain. Oh, no? While it may seem counterintuitive and sound super painful, apple cider vinegar actually takes the sting away! It can also help prevent blistering and peeling. Here's how:

¼ cup water
¼ cup apple cider vinegar
Washcloth

1. Soak the washcloth in a small bowl or basin filled with the vinegar and water.

2. Place the washcloth directly on your sunburn for 2 to 3 minutes. You should experience relief from the stinging and burning right away.

Two more ways to treat a nasty sunburn:

1. Cucumbers: The antioxidants in cucumbers may soothe swelling and pain. Place sliced, mashed, or grated cucumber directly on your skin for quick relief.
2. Aloe vera: Cut the leaf of an aloe vera plant lengthwise and squeeze the gel out directly onto burned skin.

BREATH FRESHENER

Apple cider vinegar is a great way to eliminate odors in all sorts of places: your home, your clothes, even under your arms. As it turns out, your mouth is no exception! Thanks to its antibacterial properties, apple cider vinegar is quite effective at killing germs that cause bad breath. I find that it helps get rid of what I call "onion tongue" better than gum, mints, or store-bought mouthwash, which can all be somewhat drying. For a quick fix, gargle ½ teaspoon of apple cider vinegar mixed with a cup of water. To mix up your own stash of DIY mouthwash, follow these directions:

½ cup apple cider vinegar

2 cups water

10 to 15 whole cloves (optional)

A handful of fresh mint leaves, or a few drops of peppermint oil (optional)

1. Combine all the ingredients in a jar or bottle.

2. Swish, gargle, and spit out this solution.

3. Rinse your mouth thoroughly with water.

Tip: A shot glass or old medicine cup—the kind that comes with kids' medication—makes a perfect mouthwash delivery system.

HOMEMADE AFTERSHAVE

A good aftershave does three important things: (1) it contains an antiseptic agent to keep newly shaved skin free from bacteria, (2) it soothes the skin, and (3) it helps close the pores to keep out dirt and oil. So, to make really good aftershave at home, you'd have to find something that's simultaneously antibacterial, soothing, and bracing. Hmmm, what ever could it . . . ? Hold it! By golly, the answer is again apple cider vinegar! The acetic acid in apple cider vinegar has anesthetic properties, so it eases pain should any accidental nicks happen during shaving. It also moisturizes the skin, closes the pores, and soothes razor burn. Apple cider vinegar aftershave offers everything you'd look for in a good aftershave without any weird chemicals. And with a few drops of essential oil, it's great smelling and easily customizable to your taste. Here's how:

3 tablespoons witch hazel or vodka

5 tablespoons apple cider vinegar

**A few drops of essential oil(s) of your choice
(bergamot, clove, cinnamon, grapefruit, cedarwood,
and bay are lovely, masculine scents)**

Combine all the ingredients in a small jar, close the lid, and shake to thoroughly combine. Prior to using, store the jar in a cool, dark place for 3 to 4 days, shaking it well once daily.

Tip: Consider storing your aftershave in an empty spice jar—the kind with the shaker holes in the top. This works well because you can simply shake a little bit on a cotton ball for easy application.

DANDRUFF REMEDY

Dandruff, which is actually a form of eczema, is caused by an overgrowth of a harmless, yeastlike fungus that causes scalp irritation, which, in turn, leads to scalp skin's shedding the affected cells—that is, the telltale flakes. To deal with dandruff, you've got to find a way to kill or slow the growth of fungus. Apple cider vinegar is an extremely effective way to tame the flakes. Give the following treatment a try, then dust off that black turtleneck and find the nearest coffee house, daddio:

If you experience mild dandruff

½ cup water
½ cup apple cider vinegar

Combine the water and vinegar in a squeeze bottle or spray bottle. Apply to the hair, massaging onto the scalp, then rinse. Use once a week.

If your dandruff occurs more than a few times a week

1 cup apple cider vinegar
1 cup shampoo (whatever you usually use)

Simply mix the vinegar and shampoo in a bottle or jar and use daily as you would normally use shampoo.

AT-HOME ACNE TREATMENT

Apple cider vinegar is a real heavyweight when it comes to fighting acne. Why? It kills off the bacteria that causes blemishes to rear their ugly heads, so to speak. And as we know, it also balances the pH of your skin, which makes it harder for bacteria to thrive. What's more, it's astringent and will help dry up excess oil. Combining apple cider vinegar with honey—a humectant and natural antibiotic—is a gentle yet effective way to calm and treat acne. Here's how:

2 tablespoons honey

1 tablespoon apple cider vinegar

1. In a small bowl, combine the honey and vinegar.

2. Apply to a clean face and leave on the skin for 20 minutes.

3. Rinse thoroughly with cool water. Repeat up to three times a week.

HOUSEHOLD USES

NONTOXIC ALL-PURPOSE CLEANER

I think of apple cider vinegar and water as the dynamic duo, when it comes to cleaning my home. I keep a spray bottle filled with apple cider vinegar and water under the sink in my kitchen and use it to wipe down countertops, windows, mirrors, floors, baseboards, highchairs . . . pretty much anything that'll stand still long enough for me to swipe it. The concoction is free of the kinds of nasty chemicals and petroleum found in most commercially produced cleaners that can be harmful to humans, animals, and the environment. And since I reuse the same spray bottle over and over, it creates much less packaging waste, making it both a green choice and an economical one. For the most part, I stick with a very basic formula of 2 cups water to 1 cup apple cider vinegar. But since I love the smell of lavender oil, I often add a few drops to the spray bottle, which makes the house smell like a spa (rather than the intersection of Bonkers and Diapers, which is where toddlers reside). Any essential oil works and I do mix things up from time to time. Other DIY cleaners to try:

Citrus Cleaner

2 cups citrus peels (any combination of citrus will do)
2 cups apple cider vinegar

1. Fill a mason jar halfway with the citrus peels.

2. Pour the vinegar over the peels to fill the jar.

3. Cover the jar with a lid and allow the mixture to steep in a dark place for at least 2 weeks.

4. After 2 weeks, strain the mixture into a bowl and discard the peels. Transfer to a spray bottle and use as you would any cleaner.

Tip: Want to take your cleaner to the next level? Toss in a few sprigs of fresh herbs or some whole spices. Rosemary and cloves both smell fantastic with citrus!

Heavy-Duty Bacteria-Fighting Cleaner

1 cup water
1 cup apple cider vinegar
20 drops of oregano oil

Combine the water, vinegar, and oregano oil in a spray bottle. Replace the cap and shake vigorously. Use as you would any other all-purpose cleaner for wood, glass, stainless steel, and porcelain. Wipe with a microfiber cloth or paper towel.

Note: Oregano oil is a strong germ fighter and has been shown to be effective against bacteria, including *Staphylococcus* and *E. coli*!

WANT TO TURN AN EMPTY APPLE CIDER VINEGAR BOTTLE INTO A GLASS SPRAY BOTTLE?

Simply fit the nozzle from an old spray bottle on the empty bottle's screw top and . . . voilà: reusable, BPA free, and dishwasher safe!

GENTLE CARPET CLEANER

There's a white rug in our eighteen-month-old's bedroom. It's bordered in pastels, but the majority of the rug is white. Clean, bright, white. Am I a raving lunatic for putting a white rug in a toddler's room? Perhaps I am. But, in my defense, it was a gift and it just sort of works with the ladybug motif on her walls. I know what you're thinking and, yes, of course it has taken a beating. Everything you can think of has been spilled, smeared, and ground into that thing at some point. It needs to be cleaned on a pretty regular basis. But, because it's where my little one plays, reads, rolls around, and gets dressed, I don't want to use the chemical-laden, weapons-grade cleaners that are out there. Thankfully, apple cider vinegar works really well as a carpet cleaner. For stains, spills, even odors, here's what to do:

2 cups apple cider vinegar

2 cups warm water

Baking soda

1. First, if possible, get to the mess right away and, using a rag or paper towel, blot (don't rub) as much of it as you can.

2. Then, in a bowl or pitcher, mix the vinegar and water, and pour the mixture generously over the dirty area.

3. Let the mixture go deep down into the fibers of the carpet. Blot well, then let it dry. (A fan can speed up the process.)

4. Once dry, sprinkle a good amount of baking soda over the entire section. Allow it to settle for about 15 minutes and then vacuum it off.

EARTH-FRIENDLY ROOM DEODORIZER

I'll admit it. Sometimes my house has what can only be described as that not-so-fresh feeling. (I'm sure it happens to your house, too.) There'll be a funk in the air—maybe from something you've cooked or from one too many diaper changes or from your dog's coming in from the rain or a long musty winter or—the worst—from something completely unidentifiable. Whatever the reason, I've found that you can actually clear that smell right up with nothing more than a bowl of apple cider vinegar. You don't even need to spray it around! Simply place a bowl of apple cider vinegar in the corner of the smelly room. After a few hours, the odor will be gone! Magic.

If you prefer a room spray, try this one

4 tablespoons apple cider vinegar

3 cups water

4 drops lavender essential oil (or another scent of your choice)

Combine all the ingredients in a spray bottle. Shake vigorously to combine. Spray when the air is stale or when you wish to eliminate an unpleasant odor.

FRAGRANCE-FREE FABRIC SOFTENER

Apple cider vinegar is the fabric softener of choice for many a natural, green household. In addition to being free from harsh chemicals, artificial fragrances, and . . . well, talking teddy bears . . . apple cider vinegar removes detergent buildup in the dryer and helps with static cling. Most important, it really, truly softens the laundry. And once dry, the vinegar scent completely dissipates, leaving you with nothing but clean-smelling clothes and linens.

½ cup apple cider vinegar

For average loads, add the vinegar directly into the fabric softener dispenser of your washing machine or to the rinse cycle. For larger loads, use as much as ¾ cup of vinegar.

ORGANIC FERTILIZER AND WEED KILLER

While I love to garden, weeding is pretty high on my list of "household chores that make me whine," right behind unloading the dishwasher and putting away the laundry. I wish I could be all zen about it and surrender myself to the process, but I find weeding to be monotonous, hot, and tedious. Unfortunately, most commercial herbicides contain harmful chemicals, namely glyphosate, which I just don't feel comfortable using around my family and the neighborhood pets. Toxic chemicals make me even whinier. So, what's a lazy gardener to do? Use apple cider vinegar, of course! At 5 percent acidity, undiluted apple cider vinegar zaps weeds naturally—it's reasonably safe for the environment and surprisingly effective. What's more, when diluted or doctored a bit with a few other household ingredients, apple cider vinegar can be added to garden soil or sprayed on plants to help them flourish. Here's how:

To kill weeds

1 to 2 cups apple cider vinegar, or more, as needed

Simply pour the undiluted vinegar onto garden weeds. This works especially well on garden pathways and in the cracks and crevices of sidewalks and driveways. Note: Don't assume vinegar knows which plants you want to kill; spray or pour *carefully* only where you want to get rid of weeds or risk harming your plants.

To add nutrients to plants

1 cup apple cider vinegar

1 cup sugar

1 gallon water

Combine the vinegar, sugar, and water in a watering can. Stir well and water your plants with the solution.

To make soil acidic

1 cup apple cider vinegar

1 gallon water

Combine the water and vinegar in a watering can. Mix well, then sprinkle the solution over the soil surrounding acid-loving plants, such as azaleas, rhododendrons, hydrangeas, and gardenias.

5 MORE USES FOR APPLE CIDER VINEGAR IN THE GARDEN

1. Clean stains and white mineral crusts off flowerpots by soaking them for an hour in a solution of half-water and half–apple cider vinegar.

2. Get rid of rust on gardening tools, spigots, and sprinklers by soaking them overnight or for several days in undiluted apple cider vinegar.

3. Keep bunnies from nibbling your plants. Put a rag soaked in apple cider vinegar in a plastic container with a lid (old takeout containers or yogurt tubs work well). Poke a hole in the top and place in the garden.

4. Clean plastic patio furniture with a solution of 1 tablespoon of apple cider vinegar to 1 gallon of water.

5. Remove berry or fruit stains from your hands by soaking them in apple cider vinegar.

ALL-NATURAL FRUIT FLY TRAP

We have a great year-round farmers' market in town and we try to shop there as often as we can, especially in summer. I get giddy with the arrival of all the beautiful summer produce, particularly cherries, berries, peaches, plums, and tomatoes, all of which are best stored at room temperature, not in the fridge. I used to panic when the inevitable infestation of fruit flies would begin a few weeks into summer, but I've discovered a tried-and-true remedy that gets rid of those minuscule pests before I lose my mind.

2 tablespoons apple cider vinegar
1 to 2 drops liquid dish soap

1. Pour the vinegar into the bottom of a small glass jar.

2. Add the liquid dish soap.

3. Cover the jar with plastic wrap and poke a few holes in the top.

4. Reclaim your kitchen and your sanity!

6 TIPS FOR PREVENTING FRUIT FLIES

1. Rinse fruit as soon as you get home from the market.

2. Keep the kitchen sink very clean; rinse the drain with vinegar and baking soda every few days.

3. Take the trash out daily.

4. Wash dishes right away, and, if possible, avoid leaving pots and pans to soak in the sink.

5. Don't overwater houseplants.

6. Regularly change the water in vases of cut flowers.

DIY FLORAL ARRANGEMENT PRESERVATIVE

Cut flowers, whether purchased from the florist or snipped from your own garden, are a simple pleasure and the quickest and easiest way I can think of to add life to any room. To ensure that your blooms stick around long enough for you to truly enjoy them, they need food, water, and a clean environment. To keep them looking fresh longer or to add life to droopy ones, try this:

2 tablespoons apple cider vinegar

2 tablespoons sugar

2 cups water, or more, as your vase requires

Combine the vinegar and sugar, then pour into the vase water before adding your flowers. Change the water (adding more vinegar and sugar) every 2 to 3 days, to preserve your flowers' longevity.

5 MORE TRICKS FOR EXTENDING THE LIFE OF YOUR FLOWERS

1. Put flowers in water ASAP to hydrate them.

2. Cut stems at an angle with a sharp, clean pair of clippers—it provides a wider surface for water to travel up the stem.

3. Trim your stems so that the flowers are about two thirds the height of the total arrangement, to allow the vase to properly support them.

4. Don't allow leaves or other foliage to fall beneath the water line. Otherwise, they'll create a bacterial buildup and promote mold.

5. Choose flowers with an especially long vase life, such as alstroemeria, aster, celosia, cosmos, gypsophila, lavatera, rudbeckia, scabiosa, snapdragon, statice, sunflower, yarrow, and zinnia.

CUTTING BOARD CLEANER

Wooden cutting boards are often one of a home cook's most treasured kitchen tools. Sturdy, weathered, and worn, a well-used wooden cutting board is a thing of beauty. But like any hardworking kitchen utensil, wooden boards need to be treated with a dose of respect to keep them in good working order. Washing them with soap and water damages the board over time, resulting in swollen, rough wood, which won't grip your knife well or provide a steady surface for chopping. And forget about ever putting a wooden board in the dishwasher! You're pretty much guaranteed to end up with a warped, cracked, dried-out hunk of formerly beautiful wood. Luckily, cleaning wooden cutting boards naturally and gently is easy, thanks to your new best friend: apple cider vinegar. The acetic acid in the vinegar is an excellent disinfectant, powerful against such harmful bacteria as *E. coli*, *Salmonella*, and *Staphylococcus*. To clean and sanitize your cutting board:

¼ cup apple cider vinegar

2 tablespoons baking soda

1. Wipe your cutting board down with the undiluted vinegar after each use. The vinegar smell will dissipate as the wood dries.

2. When your wooden board needs deodorizing (Garlic? What garlic!?), sprinkle some baking soda over the surface of the board, then spray on the undiluted

vinegar. Allow it foam for 5 minutes, then wipe clean with a damp cloth or sponge.

Tip: To save a wooden cutting board that someone in your house threw in the dishwasher, despite explicit instructions to wash by hand (ahem), simply sand lightly with fine-grit sandpaper, then oil with mineral oil—found at most drugstores— or olive oil.

FRUIT AND VEGETABLE WASH

Fruits and vegetables—even the organic stuff—should be washed before you eat them to remove residue from pesticides and herbicides. Also, think about how many pairs of hands touch that produce before it reaches your kitchen. Gross. Do you think everyone on the farm—all the packers, the grocery store associates, and all the other customers who handled that produce before you—had clean hands? Probably not. Also, bugs. Blech. It's better to not think about it. Just clean your produce. Here's how:

1 cup apple cider vinegar

1. Fill a clean sink halfway with lukewarm water. Add the vinegar.

2. Add your fruit and/or vegetables and soak for about 10 minutes (less time for fragile berries—2 to 5 minutes). Rinse well.

Note: Bacteria, such as *Listeria*, *Salmonella*, and *E. coli*, can all find a home on your fruits and vegetables, both conventional and organic. These are the bacteria that cause food-borne illness. Just because you can't see them doesn't mean they aren't there.

ACKNOWLEDGMENTS

To my agent Sharon Bowers: Thank you for your wise counsel, encouraging me to follow my gut, and holding my hand so many times during this process. What a pleasure it is to work with you!

To Ann Treistman: Thank you for giving me the creative freedom to make this book my own and for finding ways to make it better. I've truly enjoyed our collaboration. And huge thanks to the rest of the team at The Countryman Press, including Sarah Bennett, Devorah Backman, Natalie Eilbert, and Devon Zahn.

Thank you to Jenna Helwig, my friend and colleague, who has opened many doors and shared so much. You and I both know this book would not have happened without you and your generosity.

To Chef Ted Siegel, you gave me the technique to back up my passion. I am forever grateful for the tight ship you run, even if that means I still hear your voice in my head every time I dice potatoes. Every. Single. Time.

Thank you to my family and friends for motivating me and cheering me on. Special thanks to my parents for a lifetime of unconditional love and support; and to my in-laws, brother, and brother- and sister-in-law—each of you has helped me in your own special way. Thank you.

To my husband: Thank you for giving me the love, support, and encouragement to take on this project even though only a crazy person would attempt to write a cookbook with a toddler and preschooler at her heels day and night. I couldn't have asked for a better collaborator, in-house editor, friend, or cheerleader. Thank you for your patience, pushing me when I needed it, and your honesty (especially when literally bathing in vinegar!). I wouldn't be doing this thing that I love were it not for you. I love you.

And finally, to my sweet little girls. You make everything taste better. I love you so very much.

INDEX

Carpet Cleaner, Gentle, 154–55
carrots
Cabbage and Carrot Salad
with Peanuts, Asian Shredded, 74
Maple Bourbon Carrot and
Parsnip Pickles, 98–99
in Mexican-Style Pickled Vegetables, 90–91
cheese. *See* feta; mozzarella;
ricotta
chiles
habanero, in Fire Cider,
108–9
jalapeño, in Mexican-Style
Pickled Vegetables, 90–91
red, in Grilled Zucchini with
Chiles, Mint, and Apple
Cider Vinegar, 65–66
red, in Perfect Tomato Salad,
68–69
Chimichurri Sauce, 36–37
Chipotle Mustard, 50
chocolate, in Apple Cider Vinegar
Oatmeal Cookies, 138–39
Chocolate Bundt Cake, Eggless,
136–37
Chutney, Rhubarb, 56–57
Chutney 4 Ways, 51–57
Cider Dijon Dressing, 31
cilantro, in Mexican-Style
Pickled Vegetables, 90–91
Cinnamon-Apple Shrub,
Autumn, 116–17

Cinnamon Sugar Coating, 134
citrus, in Sparkling Honey Ade,
106
See also limes; oranges; lemons
Citrus Cleaner, 152
cleaners, household. *See under*
household uses
coconut, in Homemade Sports
Drink, 110
coconut, in Rise and Shine Straw-
berry Smoothie, 119–21
Cold and Cough Syrup, Homemade, 17
constipation remedy, 21
Cookies, Apple Cider Vinegar
Oatmeal, 138–39
cooking with vinegar
benefits and uses, 27
recipes (*see* baked and
griddle treats; beverages;
dressings, sauces, and marinades; pickles; salads)
Cough and Cold Syrup, Homemade, 17
Crab Salad with Apples and
Chives, 75
cranberries
Cranberry Chutney, 53
in Spiced Berry Warmer,
124–25
Winter Cranberry-Orange
Shrub, 118–19
Crazy Cake. *See* Eggless Chocolate Bundt Cake